The Passing Throng

By
Edgar A. Guest

Verse—
The Passing Throng
A Heap o' Livin'
Just Folks
The Path to Home
Poems of Patriotism
When Day Is Done
Rhymes of Childhood

Illustrated—
All That Matters

Prose—
Making the House a Home
My Job as a Father

The
Passing Throng

By

Edgar A. Guest

The Reilly & Lee Co.
Chicago

To

W. F. L.

Whose friendship needs neither
symbol nor token,
this book is affectionately dedicated

Birthday Greetings

Hermon

from

Betty
'28

INDEX

Index

Index

The Passing Throng

From newsboy to the millionaire
  The passing throng goes by each day;
The old man with his weight of care,
  The maiden in her colors gay,
The mother with her babe in arms,
  The dreamer and the man of might,
Grief's cruel scars and laughter's charms
  Pass by the window, day and night.

Now slowly rides a corpse to find
  The grave and its unbroken sleep,
And in the carriages behind
  A score of sorrowing loved ones weep;
But scarcely has the hearse passed by
  Upon its journey to the tomb,
When, wreathed with smiles of love, we spy
  The faces of a bride and groom.

We cannot understand it all,
  We cannot know why this is so;
From dawn until night's curtains fall,
  We see the people come and go.

Hope lights the eyes of youth to-day,
　To-morrow care has left them dim;
Once this man proudly walked his way,
　But now defeat has broken him.

Could we but watch, as God must do,
　We'd see the struggling youth arise,
We'd see him brave his dangers through,
　And reach his goal and claim the prize.
And we might judge with gentler sight
　The broken lives, which come and go,
And better choose 'twixt wrong and right —
　If we could know what God must know.

Wife o' Mine

Wife o' Mine, day after day
Cheering me along the way;
Patient, tender, smiling, true,
Always ready to renew
Faltering courage and to share
All the day may bring of care;
Dreaming dreams wherein you see
Brighter years that are to be;
Calling paltry pleasures fine —
That's you always, Wife o' Mine.

Wife o' Mine, we've shed some tears
With the passing of the years,
Mourned beside our lovely dead;
But somehow you've always said
You and I could bear the blow
Knowing God had willed it so;
And you've smiled to show to me
Just how brave you meant to be,
Smiled to keep my faith in line —
That's you, always, Wife o' Mine.

Wife o' Mine, long years ago
Once I promised you would know
Luxuries and costly things,
Gowns of silk and jeweled rings,
And you laughed as though you knew
Dreams like that could not come true;

Now perhaps they never will,
But I see you laughing still,
Welcoming me with eyes that shine —
That's you always, Wife o' Mine.

Let's Be Brave

Let's be brave when the laughter dies
And the tears come into our troubled eyes,
Let's cling to the faith and the old belief
When the skies grow gray with the clouds of
      grief,
Let's bear the sorrow and hurt and pain
And wait till the laughter comes again.

Let's be brave when the trials come
And our hearts are sad and our lips are dumb,
Let's strengthen ourselves in the times of test
By whispering softly that God knows best;
Let us still believe, though we cannot know,
We shall learn sometime it is better so.

Let's be brave when the joy departs,
Till peace shall come to our troubled hearts,
For the tears must fall and the rain come down
And each brow be pressed to the thorny crown;
Yet after the dark shall the sun arise,
So let's be brave when the laughter dies.

Boy or Girl?

Some folks pray for a boy, and some
For a golden-haired little girl to come.
  Some claim to think there is more of joy
  Wrapped up in the smile of a little boy,
  While others pretend that the silky curls
  And plump, pink cheeks of the little girls
  Bring more of bliss to the old home place
  Than a small boy's queer little freckled face.

Now which is better, I couldn't say
If the Lord should ask me to choose to-day;
  If He should put in a call for me
  And say: "Now what shall your order be,
  A boy or girl? I have both in store —
  Which of the two are you waiting for?"
  I'd say with one of my broadest grins:
  "Send either one, if it can't be twins."

I've heard it said, to some people's shame,
They cried with grief when a small boy came,
  For they wanted a girl. And some folks I
      know
  Who wanted a boy, just took on so
  When a girl was sent. But it seems to me
  That mothers and fathers should happy be
  To think, when the Stork has come and gone,
  That the Lord would trust them with either
      one.

15

Boy or girl? There can be no choice;
There's something lovely in either voice.
  And all that I ask of the Lord to do
  Is to see that the mother comes safely through
  And guard the baby and have it well,
  With a perfect form and a healthy yell,
  And a pair of eyes and a shock of hair.
  Then, boy or girl — and its dad won't care.

They're Waiting Over There

  They're waiting for us over there;
  The young, the beautiful and fair
  Who left us, oh, so long ago,
  Lonely and hurt on earth below,
  Are waiting bravely, never fear,
  Until our faces shall appear.

  Then, when our journey here is done,
  And we set out to follow on
  Through the great, heavy mantled door
  Which leads to rest forevermore,
  They will be there to laugh away
  'The loneliness we feel to-day.

  They'll welcome us with wondrous grace,
  And show us all about the place;
  They'll take us gently by the hand

And guide us through that radiant land;
They'll tell us all they've learned and seen
Through the long absence that has been.

We'll meet the friends who have been kind
To them the while we stayed behind —
Angels who long have dwelt above,
Who welcomed them with arms of love,
And sheltered them the long years through,
Just as we'd prayed for them to do.

Though now you mourn, who stay behind,
How sad 'twould be to leave, and find
Upon that distant other shore
No loved one who had gone before —
The gates of Heaven to enter through
With no one there to welcome you.

As now, when some long journey ends
And we're received by smiling friends
Who've watched and waited for our train,
So shall they welcome us again;
The young, the beautiful and fair
Will all be waiting for us there.

Visitors

We've had a lot of visitors, it seems, for weeks
    an' weeks,
And Pa is gettin' all run down. Ma says that
    when he speaks
He isn't civil any more. He mopes around the
    place
And always seems to wear a look of sadness
    on his face.
And yesterday he said to Ma when she began
    to fuss:
" I wonder when they're going to quit an' leave
    the home to us.

" It's nice to have your people come, but some
    of them should go;
Instead of that they're sticking here like bull dogs
    at a show.
' The more the merrier,' they shout, as other
    ones drop in.
I'm getting so I cannot stand to see your cousins
    grin
And, what is more, I'm getting tired of driving
    folks about
And mighty tired of visitors who must be taken
    out.

"Night after night when I've come home I've
      hauled them near and far,
You'd think I was the driver of a town sight-
      seeing car.
I've hauled them up to factories and monuments
      and parks,
Museums and aquariums; I've shown 'em seals
      and sharks
And bears and wolves and elephants; and now
      I want to quit.
I know they'd do the same for me, but I am sick
      of it.

"I wouldn't say a word at all about your folks,
      I know
They're just as nice as they can be, but still
      I wish they'd go.
I'm tired of all the buzz and talk, the tales of
      those who've died;
I'm tired of seeing all our chairs forever occu-
      pied."

"And I am tired myself," said Ma, "as tired as
      I can be,
You're only on the job at night, but it's all day
      long for me."

When Father Broke His Arm

Pa never gets a story straight.
He's always mixed about the date,
Or where it was, or what occurred,
Or who related what he heard;
And every time he starts to tell
Some little story he knows well,
Ma says: "No, Pa, as I recall,
That isn't how it was at all."

"Remember when I broke my arm,"
Says Pa, "when we were on the farm
And I went out that slippery morn
A few days after Bud was born,
To get some wood" — and Ma says then:
"Oh, Pa, don't tell that tale again!
And anyhow, I know right well
Bud wasn't born the day you fell."

"'Twas months before he came," says Ma.
"'Twas after he was born," says Pa;
"I rather think I ought to know
Just when it was I suffered so."
"Maybe you ought," says Ma, "but still,
I saw you tumble down the hill,
And it was March with snow drifts high —
Bud wasn't born till next July."

"I'd walk him round the floor," says Pa.
"You're all mixed up again," says Ma.
"We'll ask Aunt Lizzie, she was there,
She'd come to help." Says Ma: "I swear
You're just as crazy as a loon,
Aunt Lizzie didn't come till June.
To argue on is most absurd,
Bud wasn't born when that occurred."

I wish I knew just what is what
Or whether I was born or not,
But I'll just have to sit and wait
Until Pa gets his story straight;
And I have never heard at all
Just how it was he chanced to fall,
For Pa and Ma can't yet agree
Which one came first — the fall or me.

The Spirit of the Home

Dishes to wash and clothes to mend,
    And always another meal to plan,
Never the tasks of a mother end
    And oh, so early her day began!
Floors to sweep and the pies to bake,
And chairs to dust and the beds to make.

Oh, the home is fair when you come at night
    And the meal is good and the children gay,

And the kettle sings in its glad delight
    And the mother smiles in her gentle way;
So great her love that you seldom see
Or catch a hint of the drudgery.

Home, you say, when the day is done,
    Home to comfort and peace and rest;
Home, where the children romp and run—
    There is the place that you love the best!
Yet what would the home be like if you
Had all of its endless tasks to do?

Would it be home if she were not there,
    Brave and gentle and fond and true?
Could you so fragrant a meal prepare?
    Could you the numberless duties do?
What were the home that you love so much,
Lacking her presence and gracious touch?

She is the spirit of all that's fair;
    She is the home that you think you build;
She is the beauty you dream of there;
    She is the laughter with which it's filled—
She, with her love and her gentle smile,
Is all that maketh the home worth while.

If I Were Sending My Boy Afar

If I were sending my boy afar
To live and labor where strangers are,
I should hold him close till the time to go,
Telling him things which he ought to know;
I should whisper counsel and caution wise.
Hinting of dangers which might arise,
And tell him the things I have learned from life.
Of its bitter pain and its cruel strife
And the sore temptations which men beset,
And then add this: "Boy, don't forget
When your strength gives out and your hope
  grows dim,
Your father will help if you'll come to him."

If I were sending a boy away,
I should hold him close on the parting day
And give him my trust. Through thick and thin
I should tell him I counted on him to win,
To keep his word at whatever cost,
To play the man though his fight be lost.
But beyond all that I should whisper low:
"If trouble comes, let your father know;
Come to him, son, as you used to do
When you were little — he'll see you through.
I am trusting you in a distant land.
You trust your father to understand.

"Trust me wherever you chance to be,
Know there is nothing to hide from me,
Tell me it all — your tale of woe,
The sting of failure that hurts you so.
Never, whatever your plight may be,
Think it something to hide from me;
Come to me first in your hour of need,
Come though you know that my heart will bleed!
Boy, when the shadows of trouble fall,
Come to your father first of all."

The White Oak

The white oak keeps its leaves till spring when
    other trees are bare,
And who will take the time to look, will find the
    young bud there;
The young bud nestled snug and warm against
    the winter's cold;
The young bud being sheltered by the knowledge
    of the old.

And when the spring shall come again — and
    gentle turns the day,
The youthful bud will swell with strength and
    thrust the old away;
The youthful bud will seek the breeze and hunger
    for the sun,
And down to earth will fall the old with all its
    duty done.

Then, heedless of the parent leaf, the youthful
bud will grow
And watch the robins build their nests and watch
the robins go.
Then something strange will come to it when
that young leaf grows old,
It, too, will want to shield its babe against the
winter's cold.

It, too, will cling unto the tree through many a
dreary day
Until the spring-time comes again and it is thrust
away;
Then it will flutter down to earth with all its
duty done,
And leave behind its happy child to drink the
morning sun.

How like man's life from birth to close! How
like the white oak tree
Which keeps a shelter for its young against the
storms, are we!
We guard our children through the night and
watch them through the day,
And when at last our work is done, like leaves,
we fall away.

Dirty Hands

I have to wash myself at night before I go to bed,
An' wash again when I get up, and wash before
    I'm fed,
An' Ma inspects my neck an' ears an' Pa my
    hands an' shirt —
They seem to wonder why it is that I'm so fond
    of dirt.
But Bill — my chum — an' I agree that we have
    never seen
A feller doing anything whose hands were white
    an' clean.

Bill's mother scolds the same as mine an' calls
    him in from play
To make him wash his face an' hands a dozen
    times a day.
Dirt seems to worry mothers so. But when the
    plumber comes
To fix the pipes, it's plain to see he never scrubs
    his thumbs;
His clothes are always thick with grease, his face
    is smeared with dirt,
An' he is not ashamed to show the smudges on
    his shirt.

The motorman who runs the car has hands much
    worse than mine,
An' I have noticed when we ride there's dirt in
    every line.
The carpenter who works around our house can
    mend a chair
Or put up shelves or fix the floor, an' mother
    doesn't care
That he's not in his Sunday best; she never
    interferes
An' makes him stop his work to go upstairs to
    wash his ears.

The fellers really doing things, as far as I can see,
Have hands and necks and ears that are as dirty
    as can be.
The man who fixes father's car when he can't
    make it go,
Most always has a smudgy face — his hands
    aren't white as snow.
But I must wash an' wash an' wash while every-
    body knows
The most important men in town have dirty
    hands and clo'es.

If I Were a Boss

If I were a boss I would like to say:
"You did a good job here yesterday."
I'd look for a man, or a girl, or boy
Whose heart would leap with a thrill of joy
At a word of praise, and I'd pass it out
Where the crowd could hear as I walked about.

*If I were the boss I would like to find
The fellow whose work is the proper kind;
And whenever to me a good thing came,
I'd ask to be told the toiler's name,
And I'd go to him and I'd pat his back
And I'd say: "That was perfectly splendid,
      Jack!"

Now a bit of praise isn't much to give,
But it's dear to the hearts of all who live;
And there's never a man on this good old earth
But is glad to be told that he's been of worth;
And a kindly word when the work is fair
Is welcomed and wanted everywhere.

If I were a boss, I am sure I should
Say a kindly word whenever I could,
For the man who has given his best by day
Wants a little more than his weekly pay;
He likes to know, with the setting sun,
That his boss is pleased with the work he's done.

To the Little Baby

You know your mother — that's plain as day,
But those wide blue eyes of you seem to say
When I bend over your crib: "Now who
Are you?"
It's little figure I cut, I know,
And faces trouble a baby so,
But I'm the gladdest of all the glad —
Your dad!

You're two months old, and you see us smile,
And I know you are wondering all the while
Whoever on earth can these people be
You see.
You've learned your mother; you know her well
When hunger rattles the dinner bell,
But somehow or other you cannot place
My face.

As yet, I'm but one of the passing throng,
The curious people who come along
And pause at your crib, and you seem to say
Each day:
"I know one voice that is sweet to hear,
I know her step when my mother's near,
I know her wonderful smile — but who
Are you?

" You always come with the same old grin,
Your finger's rough when you tickle my chin,
But you run away when I start to cry,
And I
Don't understand when visitors call
Why you're so afraid they will let me fall.
You are the queerest of all the queer
Folks here! "

It's true that over your crib I stand
And tickle your chin with my rough old hand.
And I run away when you start to cry,
But I
Have a right to my queer little funny ways,
To boast your worth and to sound your praise,
For I am the gladdest of all the glad —
Your dad.

His Work

There isn't much fame on a farm, an' the farm
    doesn't pile up the wealth;
It gives you an appetite early an' late, an' it's
    usually lavish with health.
The world travels by in its cars, but the men and
    the women don't see
Any reason to cheer anything that I do or pin
    any medals on me;
But I'm doin' my work just the same an' at night-
    time the Lord an' I know

That the wheat's lookin' fine in the acres out
there, and I — well, I helped it to grow.

Sometimes I get gloomy an' blue an' wish I could
rise with the great,
An' wish I could point something out which my
hands have builded or helped to create;
Then the orchard looks over to me an' the fruit-
laden trees seem to say,
" If it were not for you an' the care that you've
given, we wouldn't be bearin' today."
An' the acres of corn over there, I planted 'em
all, row by row,
" The good gift o' nature," the poets declare --
but the Lord knows I helped it to grow.

I reckon I'm fillin' my place, though workin' all
day on the soil
An' standin' the heat of the merciless sun isn't
listed as glorious toil.
There's little of brilliance here, an' there's nothin'
to brag of; I guess
A farmer's a farmer, an' that's all he is — an'
his crops are his only success.
But the Lord knows, an' I know it, too, as I
plough or I harrow or hoe,
That these fields would be barren of wheat an'
of corn, if I hadn't helped 'em to grow.

Bread and Butter

I've eaten chicken a la king
    And many a fancy dish,
I think I've tasted everything
    The heart of man can wish;
But nightly when we dine alone,
    My grateful praise I utter
Unto that good old stand-by, known
    As mother's bread and butter.

Some think it very common fare
    And may be they are right,
But I can take that wholesome pair
    At morning, noon and night;
And there's a happy thrill I feel
    That sets my heart a-flutter
As I sit down to make a meal
    Of mother's bread and butter.

Though poets sing their favorite foods
    In lilting lines and sweet,
And each unto his different moods
    Tells what he likes to eat,
I still remain the little boy
    Who gleefully would mutter
A youngster's gratitude and joy
    For mother's bread and butter.

So now, for all the joy I've had
  From such a wholesome pair
Since first I was a little lad
  In hunger's deep despair,
I hold the finest food of all —
  Though epicures may sputter
And sneer me from the banquet hall —
  Is mother's bread and butter.

The Little Clothes Line

The little clothes line by the kitchen door!
  My mother stretched it once when I was young,
And there the garments which the baby wore,
  Each morning, very carefully, she hung.

Square bits of flannel fluttered in the breeze,
  White stockings very delicate and small,
Long flowing dresses and the glad bootees,
  A little blanket and a knitted shawl.

Then came the day when mother took it down,
  And we forgot what symbols fluttered there;
We'd grown to breast the current of the town,
  To fight for conquest and to stand to care.

Ten years ago she smiled and said to me:
  " I want a little clothes line by the door."
And there she hung, for all the world to see,
  The various bits of raiment which he wore.

Even the ragman on his alley round
  Knew, by the symbols fluttering on that line,
That there a little baby would be found,
  And day by day he saw that glorious sign.

Then boyhood came and called our babe away,
  Muscled him strong and turned his cheeks to
      brown,
Gave him the strength to run and romp and play,
  And then she took the little clothes line down.

To-day I sat beside her bed, and she
  Smiled the sweet smile of motherhood once
      more.
"When I get up again," she said to me,
  "I'll want a little clothes line by the door."

The Ballad of the Indifferent Whist Player

I am not much at the game,
  Careless the things that I do;
Those whose approval I claim
  When I attempt it, are few;
Bridge players look in dismay
  After a hand I have played,
Always they icily say:
  "Why did you lead me a spade?"

34

I, who am gentle and tame,
  Am scorned by a merciless crew;
I bear the brunt and the blame
  Whenever they mutter, " Down two!"
No matter what card I may play,
  No matter that whist's not my trade,
Always they sneeringly say:
  " Why did you lead me a spade?"

Matron, young maiden or dame,
  Brown eyes or gray eyes or blue,
Angrily treat me the same
  Recalling the cards that I drew.
Be it December or May,
  Ever she starts this tirade
With a look that's intended to slay:
  " Why did you lead me a spade?"

L'Envoi

Prince, when my soul flies away
  And my form in the cold ground is laid,
Let me rest where nobody will say:
  " Why did you lead me a spade?"

The Broken Wheel

We found the car beneath a tree.
" The steering knuckle broke," said he;
" The driver's dead; they say his wife
Will be an invalid for life.
I wonder how the man must feel
Who made that faulty steering wheel."

It seemed a curious thought, and I
Sat thinking, as the cars went by,
About the man who made the wheel
And shaped that knuckle out of steel;
I tried to visualize the scene—
The man, the steel and the machine.

Perhaps the workman never saw
An indication of the flaw;
Or, seeing it, he fancied it
Would not affect his work a bit,
And said: " It's good enough to go —
I'll pass it on. They'll never know."

" It's not exactly to my best
But it may pass the final test;
And should it break, no man can know
It was my hand that made it so.
The thing is faulty, but perhaps
We'll never hear it when it snaps."

Of course the workman couldn't see
The mangled car beneath the tree,
The dead man, and the tortured wife
Doomed to a cripple's chair for life—
His chief concern was getting by
The stern inspector's eager eye.

Perhaps he whistles on his way
Into the factory to-day
And doesn't know the ruin wrought
By just one minute's careless thought.
Yet human life is held at stake
By nearly all that toilers make.

The Tender Blossoms

"I will gather some flowers for our friend,"
    she said,
So into the garden with her I went
And stood for awhile at the rose's bed
    As she stooped to her labor of sentiment

"Why not the full blown blossom there?
    Why do you leave it and pass it by?"
Those were the questions I asked of her.
    And she answered me: "It is soon to die."

" Here is a withered and blasted rose,
   Better without it the plant would be;
Cut it and mingle it now with those
   You are taking away for your friend to see."

" Here is a peony stained and torn,
   Take it and cling to your choicest bloom."
But she answered me with a look of scorn:
   " These flowers are to brighten a sick friend's
      room."

" Only the tenderest bud I'll take.
   Never the withered and worn and old;
Of my fairest flowers is the gift I make
   By which my love for my friend is told."

" So, when the angels call," said I,
   " And fold in their arms a little child,
Passing the old and the broken by,
   Think of this and be reconciled.

" Always the tenderest buds they take,
   Pure and lovely and undefiled.
When a gift of love unto God they'd make,
   Always they come for a little child."

Questioning

You shall wonder as you meet
Drunkards reeling down the street,
Helpless cripples and the blind,
Human wrecks of every kind
Living on from day to day,
Why your loved one couldn't stay.

These are thoughts which always come
When the heart with grief is numb.
" Why," the anguished mother cries,
With the tears still in her eyes,
" Must my baby go away
And some sinful creature stay? "

Thus, rebellious in your grief,
You may falter in belief
And your blinded eyes will see
No just cause why this should be;
But the passing years will show
Wisely was it ordered so.

Hold your faith and bear the pain —
Questioning your God is vain.
None of us has power to know
Who should stay and who should go.
Hold this everlasting truth —
Heaven has need of lovely youth.

Think of this when you are tried:
If the wretched only died,
Then would death to us be sent
Always as a punishment?
But the passing from the earth
Is more beautiful than birth.

The Choir Boy

They put his spotless surplice on
  And tied his flowing tie,
And he was fair to look upon
  As he went singing by.
He sang the hymns with gentle grace,
  That little lad of nine,
For there was something in his face
  Which seemed almost divine.

His downcast eye was good to see,
  His brow was smooth and fair,
And no one dreamed that there could be
  A rascal plotting there;
Yet when all heads in prayer were bowed,
  God's gracious care to beg,
The boy next to him cried aloud:
  "Quit pinching o' my leg!"

A pious little child he seemed,
　An angel born to sing;
Beholding him, none ever dreamed
　He'd do a naughty thing;
Yet many a sudden "ouch!" proclaimed
　That he had smuggled in
For mischief-making, unashamed,
　A most disturbing pin.

And yet, I think, from high above,
　The Father looking down,
Knows everything he's thinking of
　And smiles when mortals frown,
For in the spotless surplice white
　Which is his mother's joy,
He knows he's not an angel bright,
　But just a healthy boy.

The Lay of the Troubled Golfer

His eye was wild and his face was taut with
    anger and hate and rage,
And the things he muttered were much too strong
    for the ink of the printed page.
I found him there when the dusk came down, in
    his golf clothes still was he,
And his clubs were strewn around his feet as he
    told his grief to me:
" I'd an easy five for a seventy-nine — in sight
    of the golden goal —
An easy five and I took an eight — an eight on
    the eighteenth hole!

" I've dreamed my dreams of the ' seventy men,'
    and I've worked year after year,
I have vowed I would stand with the chosen few
    ere the end of my golf career;
I've cherished the thought of a seventy score, and
    the days have come and gone
And I've never been close to the golden goal my
    heart was set upon.
But today I stood on the eighteenth tee and
    counted that score of mine,
And my pulses raced with the thrill of joy — I'd
    a five for a seventy-nine!

"I can kick the ball from the eighteenth tee and
     get this hole in five,
But I took the wood and I tried to cross that
     ditch with a mighty drive — "
Let us end the quotes, it is best for all to imagine
     his language rich,
But he topped that ball, as we often do, and the
     pill stopped in the ditch.
His third was short and his fourth was bad and
     his fifth was off the line,
And he took an eight on the eighteenth hole with
     a five for a seventy-nine.

I gathered his clubs and I took his arm and alone
     in the locker room
I left him sitting upon the bench, a picture of
     grief and gloom;
And the last man came and took his shower and
     hurried upon his way,
But still he sat with his head bowed down like
     one with a mind astray,
And he counted his score card o'er and o'er and
     muttered this doleful whine:
"I took an eight on the eighteenth hole, with a
     five for a seventy-nine!"

Peter and Paul

Peter's the fellow I go to whenever Paul presses
    his claim.
Peter is easy to deal with, Peter's not ready with
    blame;
Paul has a way of insisting I shall be true to
    my word,
And hints of a final accounting whenever a debt
    is incurred.

Peter is pleasant and smiling and ready to lend
    when he can;
Paul offers counsel and caution and talks of the
    ways of a man,
And whenever Paul's debts must be settled and
    I must return what I owe
And haven't the money I promised, to borrow
    from Peter I go.

But the more that I think about Peter, the
    greater my fancy for Paul,
I know he'd be first to defend me if ever dis-
    aster should fall,
For Peter thinks only of money and smilingly
    reckons his fee,
While Paul, when he whispers of caution, thinks
    not of himself but of me.

Paul would defend me from trouble, would
 shield and protect my renown,
But Peter would add to my burdens and smilingly let me go down.
Yes, Peter the pleasant would wreck me, and
 gloat when I rode to my fall,
So the more that I learn about Peter, the greater
 my fondness for Paul.

Life's Equipment

" Here's how I figure it out," says he,
" With my ears to hear and my eyes to see,
And my legs to walk and my hands to work,
And a head to bow and a cap to jerk
Whenever a woman I know goes by —
It's well-equipped for this life, am I.

" Kings and princes and high and low
Have noses to smell when the blossoms blow,
And eyes to see, but I don't suppose
A king smells more with his royal nose
Or sees more charm with his kingly eye
In the pink of the orchard blooms, than I.

" But eyes and ears and legs and hands
Don't always follow the same commands,
And some find beauty in dollar bills,

And some in the streams and the misty hills;
Some people hear nothing but mortal words,
And some are tuned to the songs of birds.

" Some grapple with facts that are stiff and cold,
And some see visions all tipped with gold;
Some hands are tender and others rough,
And some are gentle and some are gruff;
But each must follow life's pathway through,
Doing the things which he likes to do.

" Now I find joy when I tramp about,
Up hill and down, for my legs are stout
And my ears and eyes can pick up things
That are maybe lost to the wisest kings;
And I'm always grateful, when day is through,
That I'm built for the things which I like to do. "

A Fairy Story

Sit here on my knee, little girl, and I'll tell
  A story to you
  Of a fairy I knew
Who lived in a garden when I was a child.
She was lovely to see and whenever she smiled
The sunbeams came dancing around just to know
Whatever it was that was pleasing her so.

She lived in a poppy and used to peek out
  And shout: "Oh, Yoo-hoo!
  I've been waiting for you!"
And then I'd go over to her house and play
And she'd saddle a bee and we'd both ride away,
Or sometimes we'd take a most wonderful trip
With the sky for the sea and a cloud for our
      ship.

Oft my father and mother would look out and
      say:
  " The glad little elf
  Plays there all by himself,
And he comes in and tells us of things he has
      seen
And the marvelous places to which he has been;
He tells us of dining with princes and kings —
It's a curious boy who can think up such things."

Now this all occurred in the long years ago,
  And the fairy has fled,
  And the poppies are dead,
And never again may I ride on a bee,
Or sail on a cloud with the sky for the sea.
But that fairy has promised, when poppies are
      fair,
To come back again and to wait for you there.

Yes, you can go out when the skies are all blue
  And see what I've seen,
  And go where I've been.
You can have fairies to lead you away,
To show you strange sights and to share in your
      play;
And the grown-ups may say that your fancies
      are wild,
But fairies are real to an innocent child.

Shoes

I'll tell you it's a problem, when a youngster's
　　　　nine years old,
To keep his feet in leather and to keep him
　　　　heeled and soled;
Just about the time I fancy I've some money I
　　　　can use,
His mother comes and tells me that he needs a
　　　　pair of shoes.

Now I can wear a pair of shoes for several
　　　　months or more,
But Bud, it seems, is working for the man who
　　　　keeps the store,
And the rascal seems to fancy that his duty is
　　　　to show
How fast a healthy, rugged boy can wreck a
　　　　leather toe.

But shoes are made for romping in, for climbing
　　　　and for fun,
For kicking bricks and empty cans, and I am
　　　　not the one
To make him walk sedately in the way that
　　　　grown-ups do —
There's time enough for that, I say, when all his
　　　　boyhood's through.

So let him wreck them, heels and toes, and scuff
    their soles away,
I'll not begrudge the bill for shoes that I'm com-
    pelled to pay,
For I rejoice that it's my lot, when mother
    breaks the news,
To have a healthy, roguish boy who's always
    needing shoes.

Football

I'd rather fancied it would come, a healthy boy
    who's ten years old
Forecasts the things he'll want to do without his
    secrets being told;
And so last night when I got home and found
    his mother strangely still,
I guessed somehow that mother love had battled
    with a youngster's will.
" You'll have to settle it," said she; " there's noth-
    ing more that I can say,
The game of football's calling him and he insists
    he wants to play."

We've talked it over many a time; we've hoped
    he wouldn't choose the game,
And I suppose there's not a boy whose parents
    do not feel the same.
They dread, as we, the rugged sport; they won-
    der, too, just what they'll say

When son of theirs comes home, as ours, and
  begs to be allowed to play.
And now the question's up to me, a question
  that I can't evade,
But football is a manly game and I am glad he's
  not afraid.

He wants to play, he says to me; he knows the
  game is rough and grim,
But worse than hurt and broken bones is what
  his friends will think of him;
"They'd call me yellow," he explained, "if I
  stay out." Of all things here
There's nothing quite so hard to bear as is the
  heartless gibe or jeer,
And though I cannot spare him pain or hurt
  when tackles knock him flat,
Being his father, I've said "yes," because I choose
  to spare him that.

She Never Gave Me a Chance

It happened that I came along as school was let-
ting out
And laughing boys and smiling girls raced everywhere about;
But two there were who walked along the road
in front of me
And one young head was bowed to earth, a
troubled lad was he;
And as I stepped around the pair to hasten on
my way:
" She never gave a chance to me!" I heard the
youngster say.

Oh, I have been a boy myself, and I have been
to school
And I have suffered punishment for breaking
many a rule;
I've worn the brand of mischief and been written
down as bad,
So I could reconstruct the scene — the teacher
and the lad,
The swift avenging punishment, the stern and
angry glance,
The blot of shame upon a boy sent home without
a chance.

I did not stop to ask the lad his little tale to
    tell,
There was no need of that because I knew the
    story well —
" She never gave a chance to me! " that sentence
    held it all.
A hundred times I'd lived the scene in days when
    I was small,
A broken rule, a teacher vexed, hot rage where
    calm belonged,
A guilty judgment blindly made — a youngster
    sadly wronged.

I still can see that little chap upon his homeward
    way,
" She never gave a chance to me," I still can hear
    him say,
And so I write this verse for him, and all the
    girls and boys
Who shall their tutors now and then disturb with
    needless noise.
Be fair, you teachers of our land, in every cir-
    cumstance;
Don't let some little fellow say he never had a
    chance.

Down the Lanes of August

Down the lanes of August — and the bees upon
    the wing —
All the world's in color now, and all the song
    birds sing;
Never reds will redder be, more golden be the
    gold,
Down the lanes of August, and the summer get-
    ting old.

Mother Nature's brushes now with paints are
    dripping wet,
Gorgeous is her canvas with the tints we can't
    forget;
Here's a yellow wheat field — purple asters
    there —
Riotous the colors that she's splashing every-
    where.

Red the cheeks of apples and pink the peaches'
    bloom,
Redolent the breezes with the sweetness of per-
    fume;
Everything is beauty, crowned by skies of clear-
    est blue;
Mother Earth is at her best once more for me
    and you.

Down the lanes of August, with her blossoms at
      our feet,
Rich with gold and scarlet, dripping wet with
      honey sweet.
Rich or poor, no matter, here are splendors
      spread —
Down the lanes of August, for all who wish to
      tread.

Arcady

Where is the road to Arcady,
  Where is the path that leads to peace,
Where shall I find the bliss to be,
  Where shall the weary wanderings cease?
These are the questions that come to me —
Where is the road to Arcady?

Is there a mystic time and place
  To which some day shall the traveler fare,
Where there is never a frowning face
  And never a burden hard to bear,
Where we as children shall romp and race?
Is there a mystic time and place?

For Arcady is an earthly sphere,
  Where only the gentlest breezes blow,
A port of rest for the weary here,

Where the velvet grass and the clover grow.
I question it oft, is it far or near?
For Arcady is an earthly sphere.

And the answer comes — it is very near,
    It's there at the end of a little street,
Where your children's voices are ringing clear
    And you catch the patter of little feet.
Where is the spot that is never drear?
And the answer comes — it is very near.

For each man buildeth his Arcady,
    And each man fashions his Port of Rest;
And never shall earth spot brighter be
    Than the little home that with peace is blessed.
So seek it not o'er the land and sea —
For each man buildeth his Arcady.

Sacrifices

Behind full many a gift there lies
A splendid tale of sacrifice.

On Christmas morn a mother's hand
   About a young girl's neck will place
A trinket small, and she will stand
   With radiant smiles upon her face
To see her daughter decked in gold —
   Nor will she think, nor will she care
That she may suffer from the cold
Because that bauble glistens there.

A child will wake on Christmas day
   And find his stocking filled with toys;
The home will ring with laughter gay —
   That boy be glad as richer boys.
And there a mother fond will sing
   A song of joy to hear his shout —
Forgetting every needed thing
   That she will have to do without.

A heart that's brimming o'er with love
   Will suffer gladly for a friend,
And take no time in thinking of
   How much it can afford to spend.
And suddenly on Christmas morn
   Will gladness beam from shining eyes —

A gladness that alone was born
   Of someone's willing sacrifice.

Let cynics scoff howe'er they will
   And say but fools such presents give,
There'll be such sacrifices till
   All human love shall cease to live.
'Twould be a dreary world of thrift,
   Of barren ways, and sunless skies,
If no one ever gave a gift
   That was not born of sacrifice.

The brightest gifts that us reward
Are those the givers can't afford.

The Callers

Who's dat knockin' at de do',
   Who's dat callin' here ter-day?
What yo' want to see me fo'?
   Tell me what yo' got to say.
What yo' name an' what yo' mean,
   Standin' out there in de gloam?
Trouble, waitin' to come in?
   No sir, no sir, I ain't home!

Who's dat ringin' of de bell,
  Wakin' me in dead of night,
When Ah was a-sleepin' well,
  Rousin' me wid such a fright?
What yo' name and what yo' hurry?
  Seems to me yo're actin' queer.
What's dat? Yo' is Mister Worry?
  No sir, no sir, I ain't here!

Who's dat waitin' at my do'?
  What yo' want a-hangin' round?
Ain't yo' nebber gwine ter go?
  Jes' yo' quit dat knockin' sound.
Tell me now jes' what yo' meant
  Callin' out my name dat way.
What's dat? Yo' is Discontent?
  No sir, I ain't home ter-day!

Mornin'! Howdy, Mister Smile!
  Mornin' Sunshine, how yo' do?
Ah'se been waitin' all de while
  Jes' ter get a call from you.
Walk right in an' take a seat,
  Where's yo' brudder, Joy, ter-day?
Jes' a-comin' down de street?
  Enter! Here's de place ter stay.

Giuseppe Tomassi

Giuseppe Tomassi ees stylisha chap,
    He wear da white collar an' cuff;
He says: " For expanse I no giva da rap,
    Da basta ees not good enough."
When out weeth hees Rosa he wear da silk hat,
    An' carry da cane lik' da lord;
He spenda hees money lik' dees, an' lik' dat,
    For Giuseppe, he work at da Ford.

He smoke da seegar with da beega da band,
    Da tree-for-da-quart' ees da kind;
Da diamond dat flash from da back of hees hand
    Ees da beegest Giuseppe could find.
He dress up hees Rosa in satin an' lace,
    She no longer scrub at da board,
But putta da paint on de leeps an' da face,
    For Giuseppe, he work at da Ford.

Giuseppe, ees strutta about lik' da king,
    An' laugh at da hard-worka man
Who grinda da org' a few neekels to bring,
    Or sella da ripa banan'.
Each morning he waxa da blacka moustache,
    Then walk up an' down through da ward;
You betta he gotta da playnta da cash,
    For Giuseppe, he work at da Ford.

Battle of Belleau Wood

This poem was chosen by Major General John A. Lejeune, Commandant of the United States Marine Corps, as his favorite of all the Marine Corps verse written during the war.

It was thick with Prussian troopers, it was foul
    with German guns;
Every tree that cast a shadow was a sheltering
    place for Huns.
Death was guarding every roadway, death was
    watching every field,
And behind each rise of terrain was a rapid-fire
    concealed;
Uncle Sam's Marines had orders: "Drive the
    Boche from where they're hid.
For the honor of Old Glory, take the woods!"
    And so they did.

I fancy none will tell it as the story should be
    told —
None will ever do full justice to those Yankee
    troopers bold —
How they crawled upon their stomachs through
    the fields of golden wheat,
With the bullets spitting at them in that awful
    battle heat.
It's a tale too big for writing; it's beyond the
    voice or pen,
But it glows among the splendor of the bravest
    deeds of men.

It's recorded as a battle, but I fancy it will live
As the brightest gem of courage human struggles have to give.
Inch by inch, they crawled to victory toward the
flaming mouths of guns;
inch by inch, they crawled to grapple with the
barricaded Huns;
On through fields that death was sweeping with
a murderous fire, they went
Till the Teuton line was vanquished and the Ger-
man strength was spent.

Ebbed and flowed the tides of battle, as they've
seldom done before;
Slowly, surely, moved the Yankees against all the
odds of war.
For the honor of the fallen, for the glory of the
dead,
The living line of courage kept the faith and
moved ahead.
They'd been ordered not to falter, and when night
came on they stood
With Old Glory proudly flying o'er the trees of
Belleau Wood.

Partridge Time

When Pa came home last night he had a package
    in his hand;
" Now, Ma," said he, " I've something here
    which you will say is grand.
A friend of mine got home to-day from hunting
    in the woods,
He's been away a week or two, and got back with
    the goods.
He had a corking string of birds — I wish you
    could have seen 'em ! "
" If you've brought any partridge home," said
    Ma, " you'll have to clean 'em."

" Now listen, Ma," said Pa to her, " these birds
    are mighty rare.
I know a lot of men who'd pay a heap to get a
    pair.
But it's against the law to sell this splendid sort
    of game,
And if you bought 'em you would have to use a
    different name.
It isn't every couple has a pair to eat between
    'em."
" If you got any partridge there," says Ma,
    " you'll have to clean 'em."

" Whenever kings want something fine, it's partridge that they eat,
And millionaires prefer 'em, too, to any sort of
meat.
About us everywhere to-night are folks who'd
think it fine
If on a brace of partridge they could just sit
down to dine.
They've got a turkey skinned to death, they're
sweeter than a chicken."
" If that's what you've brought home," says Ma,
" you'll have to do the pickin'."

And then Pa took the paper off and showed Ma
what he had.
" There, look at those two beauties! Don't they
start you feelin' glad?
An' ain't your mouth a-waterin' to think how fine
they'll be
When you've cooked 'em up for dinner, one for
you an' one for me?"
But Ma just turned her nose up high, an' said,
when she had seen 'em,
"You'll never live to eat 'em if you wait for me
to clean 'em."

The Making of a Friend

We nodded as we passed each day
  And smiled and went along our way;
I knew his name, and he knew mine,
  But neither of us made a sign
That we possessed a common tie;
  We barely spoke as we passed by.

How fine he was I never guessed.
  The splendid soul within his breast
I never saw. From me were hid
  The many kindly deeds he did.
His gentle ways I didn't know,
  Or I'd have claimed him long ago.

Then trouble came to me one day,
  And he was first to come and say
The cheering words I longed to hear.
  He offered help, and standing near
I felt our lives in sorrow blend —
  My neighbor had become my friend.

How many smiles from day to day
  I've missed along my narrow way;
How many kindly words I've lost,
  What joy has my indifference cost?
This glorious friend that now I know,
  Would have been friendly years ago.

Stick to It

Stick to it, boy,
   Through the thick and the thin of it!
Work for the joy
   That is born of the din of it.
Failures beset you,
But don't let them fret you;
Dangers are lurking,
But just keep on working.
If it's worth while and you're sure of the right
      of it,
Stick to it, boy, and make a real fight of it!

Stick to it, lad,
   Be not frail and afraid of it;
Stand to the gad
   For the man to be made of it.
Deaf to the sneering
And blind to the jeering,
Willing to master
The present disaster,
Stick to it, lad, through the trial and test of it,
Patience and courage will give you the best of it.

Stick to it, youth,
  Be not sudden to fly from it;
This is the truth,
  Triumph may not far lie from it.
Dark is the morning
Before the sun's dawning,
Battered and sore of it
Bear a bit more of it,
Stick to it, even though blacker than ink it is,
Victory's nearer, perhaps, than you think it is!

Proud Father

There's a smile on the face of the mother to-day,
The furrows of pain have been scattered away,
Her eyes tell a story of wondrous delight
As she looks at the baby who came through the
        night.
It's plain she's as happy and proud as can be,
  But you ought to see me!

The nurse wears her cap in its jauntiest style,
And she says: "Oh, my dear, there's a baby
        worth while!
She's the pink of perfection, as sweet as a rose,
And I never have seen such a cute little nose."
Were it proper for nurses she'd dance in her glee,
  But you ought to see me!

Bud's eyes are ablaze with the glory of joy,
And he has forgotten he'd asked for a boy.
He stands by her crib and he touches her cheek
And would bring all the kids on the street for a
peek.
Oh, the pride in his bearing is something to see,
But you ought to see me!

You may guess that the heart of the mother is
glad,
But for arrogant happiness gaze on the dad.
For the marvelous strut and the swagger of
pride,
For the pomp of conceit and the smile satisfied,
For joy that's expressed in the highest degree,
Take a good look at me!

The Mortgage and the Man

This is the tale of a mortgage and a dead man
    and his son,
A father who left to his only child a duty that
    must be done.
And the neighbors said as they gathered round
    in the neighbor's curious way:
" Too bad, too bad that he left his boy so heavy
    a debt to pay."

Day by day through the years that came, the
    mortgage held him fast —
Straight and true to his task he went, and he
    paid the debt at last;
And his arm grew strong and his eye kept bright,
    and although he never knew,
The thing that fashioned a man of him was the
    task he had to do.

Honor and fortune crowned his brow till the
    day he came to die,
But he said : " My boy shall never work against
    such odds as I.
I have planned his years, I have made them safe,
    I have paid his journey through."
And the boy looked out on a world wherein
    there was nothing for him to do.

His hands grew soft and his eyes went dull and
his cheeks turned ashy pale,
For strength which isn't employed by day, with
idleness grows stale.
" He is not the man that his father was," the
neighbors often said,
" And better for him had he been left to work
for his meat and bread."

Oh, the race dies out and the clan departs, and
feeble grows the son
When they come at last to the dreadful day when
all of the work is done.
For manhood dies on the roads of ease where
the skies are ever blue,
And each of us needs, if we shall grow strong,
some difficult thing to do.

The Training of Jimmy McBride

Jimmy McBride was a common sense lad,
The son of a common sense mother and dad
Who had borne him and bred him to labor.
He'd been taught what a common sense lad understands,
That the Lord in His wisdom had given him hands
For handling a pick or a sabre.

"Your feet are for walking," his father once said,
"To see with, God gave you two eyes in your head,
And your mouth is for eating and drinking;
And that you'll remember I'm making it plain,
You've also been given what men call a brain,
And the brain is put in there for thinking.

"Now you've all the equipment the greatest possess,
And some men have risen to glory with less,
So don't be afraid, but go to it;
If it's honest, and useful, and ought to be done,
Don't think it beneath you, but jump in, my son —
Go straight to your duty and do it."

When Jimmy came home with the dirt on his
    face
They never once said: "It's a shame and dis-
    grace!
Poor boy, you are worn out and weary!"
No pity for Jimmy his labors inspired.
His old father said: "It is sweet to be tired,
It makes the home-coming so cheery."

His old mother said with the pride in her eye,
" There's nothing like work to put flavor in pie.
Come in and sit down to your dinner."
And they said to themselves when he'd gone to
    his bed,
" He's earning his way and he's forging ahead —
Our Jimmy McBride is a winner."

And when their old age came upon them at last,
No touch of regret stole the joy from the past,
Nor envy of happier neighbor.
And they thanked the good Lord who had sent
    them their Jim
That they'd had the wisdom in dealing with him
To teach him the value of labor.

The Scoutmaster

There isn't any pay for you, you serve without
    reward;
The boys who tramp the fields with you but little
    could afford;
And yet your pay is richer far than men who
    toil for gold,
For in a dozen different ways your service shall
    be told.

You'll read it in the faces of a troop of growing
    boys,
You'll read it in the pleasure of a dozen manly
    joys;
And down the distant future—you will surely
    read it then,
Emblazoned through the service of a band of
    loyal men.

Five years of willing labor and of brothering a
    troop;
Five years of trudging highways, with the Indian
    cry and whoop;
Five years of camp fires burning, not alone for
    pleasure's sake,
But the future generation which these boys are
    soon to make.

They have no gold to give you, but when age
  comes on to you
They'll give you back the splendid things you
  taught them how to do;
They'll give you rich contentment and a thrill
  of honest pride
And you'll see your nation prosper, and you'll
  all be satisfied.

•

The Way of a Wife

She wasn't hungry, so she said. A salad and a
  cup of tea
Was all she felt that she could eat, but it was
  different with me.
" I'm rather hungry," I replied: " if you don't
  mind, I think I'll take
Some oysters to begin with and a good old-
  fashioned sirloin steak."

Now wives are curious in this; to make the
  statement blunt and straight,
There's nothing tempts their appetites like food
  upon another's plate;
And when those oysters six appeared she looked
  at them and said to me,
" Just let me try one, will you, dear?" and right
  away she swallowed three.

On came the steak, and promptly she exclaimed:
　　"Oh my, that looks so good!
I think I'd like a bit of it." The game is one I
　　understood.
I cut her off a healthy piece and never whim-
　　pered when she said:
"Now just a few potatoes, dear, and also let
　　me share your bread."

She wasn't hungry! She'd refused the food I
　　had been glad to buy,
But on the meal which came for me, I know she
　　turned a hungry eye.
She never cares for much to eat, she's dainty in
　　her choice, I'll state,
But she gets ravenous enough to eat whatever's
　　on my plate.

He'd been delivering a load of coal, and a five-
    ton truck he steered;
He wasn't a pretty sight to see with his four
    days' growth of beard.
His clothes were such as a coal man wears, and
    the fine folks passing by
Would have scorned the touch of his dirty hands
    and the look in his weary eye.

He rattled and banged along the road, sick of his
    job, no doubt,
When in front of his truck, from a hidden spot,
    a dog and a child dashed out
And he couldn't stop, so he made one leap from
    the height of his driver's seat
And he caught the child with those dirty hands
    and swept her from the street.

Over his legs went the heavy wheels, and they
    picked him up for dead,
And the rich man's wife placed her sable coat
    as a pillow for his head.
And black as he was, the rich man said: "He
    shall travel home with me."
And he sat by his side in the limousine and was
    proud of his company.

You may walk in pride in your garments fine,
    you may judge by the things of show,
But what's deep in the breast of the man you
    scorn is something you cannot know.
And you'd kiss the hand of the dirtiest man that
    ever the world has known
If to save the life of the child you love, he had
    bravely risked his own.

The Out-Doors Man

He must come back a better man,
Beneath the summer bronze and tan,
Who turns his back on city strife
To neighbor with the trees;
He must be stronger for the fight
And see with clearer eye the right,
Who fares beneath the open sky
And welcomes every breeze.

The man who loves all living things
Enough to go where Nature flings
Her glories everywhere about,
And dwell with them awhile,
Must be, when he comes back once more,
A little better than before,
A little surer of his faith
And readier to smile.

He never can be wholly bad
Who seeks the sunshine and is glad
To hear a songbird's melody
Or wade a laughing stream;
Nor worse than when he went away
Will he return at close of day
Who's chummed with happy birds and trees,
And taken time to dream.

A Book and a Pipe

Give me a book and my cozy chair and a pipe
    of old perique
And the wind may howl and I shall not care
    that the night is cold and bleak,
For I'll follow my friend of the printed page
    wherever he leads me on,
I'll follow him back to a vanished age and the
    joys of a life that's gone.

I'll stand with him on a brigantine with the
    salt wind in my face,
I'll hear him shout when the whale is seen and
    share in the stirring chase,
And I'll hear him say as the gulls fly by and
    round us overhead:
" Every bird up there with its ghastly cry is the
    soul of a sailor dead."

I'll go with him where the pole star gleams and
the arctic nights are long,
I'll go with him to his land of dreams away from
the surging throng,
I'll stand with him on the battle line where the
sky with flame turns red,
I'll follow this faithful friend of mine wherever
he wants to tread.

Oh, whether it be adventure grim or the calm of
a noble mind,
Or a sea to sail and a ship to trim or a pearl of
truth to find,
Grant me an hour in my easy chair and a pipe
full of old perique
And there's ever a friendly book up there that
can furnish the joy I seek.

The time I played with Vardon, I was surely on
 my game,
The gallery was greeting every shot with loud
 acclaim.
I was driving right with Harry, and was getting
 home in two,
And every trick that Vardon tried, I showed that
 I could do;
I had the Briton worried — I could tell it from
 his look,
For I was doing everything he'd printed in his
 book.

I'd held him level several holes, and then the
 crowd began,
In a fever of excitement, to applaud me to a
 man;
Men were whispering together, " Eddie's surely
 right today —
He is just as good as Vardon! Oh, it's great to
 watch him play!"
Then Vardon tried a long one, but his ball just
 missed the cup,
And I dropped my twenty-footer for a birdie and
 was up!

Nip-and-tuck out there we battled, and I ven-
    tured soon to guess
If I could keep it going, I'd make Mr. Vardon
    press;
He was very nice about it, but when I'd got home
    in two
I noticed he was lunging like I often used to do.
Then he dubbed a shot completely, when I'd
    played a perfect cleek,
And I whispered to my caddie: "Vardon some-
    times takes a peek!"

I was just one up on Vardon on the good old
    eighteenth tee,
And a half was all I needed for my greatest
    victory.
I was confident of winning — calm and cool
    about it, too;
I wasn't going to falter, for I knew what I
    could do.
I looked the distance over, then I made a perfect
    stroke —
But just then the missus shook me, and confound
    it! I awoke!

Teach Them of the Flag

Teach the children of the Flag,
  Let them know the joy it holds
  In its sun-kissed rippling folds;
Don't let patriotism lag:
  Train them so that they will love
  Every star and stripe above.

As you teach their lips to pray,
  Teach them always to be true
  To the red, the white and blue;
Praise the Flag from day to day,
  Tell the children at your knee
  All the joys of liberty.

Let them know and understand
  How the Flag was born and why;
  Tell how brave men went to die
Gladly for their native land;
  Whisper to them that they must
  Make the Flag their sacred trust.

Love of country ever starts
  In the home and at your knee;
  There the Flag shall come to be
Shrined in patriotic hearts;
  They shall gladly serve their land
  When they know and understand.

Being Brave at Night

The other night 'bout two o'clock, or maybe it
    was three,
An elephant with shining tusks came chasing
    after me.
His trunk was wavin' in the air an' spoutin' jets
    of steam
An' he was out to eat me up, but still I didn't
    scream
Or let him see that I was scared — a better
    thought I had,
I just escaped from where I was and crawled
    in bed with dad.

One time there was a giant who was horrible
    to see,
He had three heads and twenty arms, an' he
    come after me
And red hot fire came from his mouths and
    every hand was red
And he declared he'd grind my bones and make
    them into bread.
But I was just too smart for him, I fooled him
    mighty bad,
Before his hands could collar me I crawled in
    bed with dad.

I ain't scared of nothing that comes pesterin'
    me at night.
Once I was chased by forty ghosts all shimmery
    an' white,
An' I just raced 'em round the room an' let 'em
    think maybe
I'd have to stop an' rest awhile, when they could
    capture me.
Then when they leapt onto my bed, Oh Gee!
    but they were mad
To find that I had slipped away an' crawled in
    bed with dad.

No giants, ghosts or elephants have dared to
    come in there
'Coz if they did he'd beat 'em up and chase 'em
    to their lair.
They just hang 'round the children's rooms an'
    snap an' snarl an' bite
An' laugh if they can make 'em yell for help
    with all their might,
But I don't ever yell out loud. I'm not that sort
    of lad,
I slip from out the covers and I crawl in bed
    with dad.

A Cup of Tea

Nellie made a cup of tea,
Made and poured it out for me,
And above the steaming brew
Smiled and asked me: " One or two? "
Saucily she tossed her head,
" Make it sweet for me," I said.

Two sweet lumps of sugar fell
Into that small china well,
But I knew the while I drained
Every drop the cup contained,
More than sugar in the tea
Made the beverage sweet for me.

This to her I tried to say
In that golden yesterday —
Life is like a cup of tea
Which Time poureth endlessly,
Brewed by trial's constant heat,
Needing love to make it sweet.

Then I caught her looking up,
And I held my dainty cup
Out to her and bravely said:
" Here is all that lies ahead,
Here is all my life to be —
Will you make it sweet for me? "

That was years ago, and now
There is silver in her brow;
We have sorrowed, we have smiled,
We've been hurt and reconciled —
But whatever had to be,
She has made it sweet for me.

The Inspiration of the Past

When melancholy rides the sky and fills
    The distance with her dust of gloom and
        doubt,
    And from despair there seems no gateway out;
When the cold blast of disappointment chills
The green young buds of hope and the once rosy
        hills
    Stand gaunt, forbidding battlements, too stout
For faltering strength to master, ere it kills
    Faith in high purpose, turn your face about.

Search the great past, the ages that have gone;
    Pause and reflect by some remembered grave;
At Valley Forge once more with Washington,
    Learn what it means to suffer and be brave.
Or stand with patient Lincoln and believe
That what is right, its purpose shall achieve.

The Waiter

I met him in a college town, a youngster with a
    grin,
And he was sweeping up the floor when I was
    ushered in.
When I had registered my name, he put aside
    his broom
To grab my suitcase from the floor and show me
    to my room.

That night at dinner I beheld that youngster at
    my side,
"We've pork and lamb," said he to me, "pota-
    toes, baked or fried."
When I had made my choice of food, he gayly
    went away
And when he next appeared he had my dinner
    on a tray.

"So you're a waiter too?" said I. He chuckled
    soft and low:
"Three times a day it is my job the dishes
    round to throw.
I'm bell hop in the afternoons, between times
    I'm the clerk,
But I can get my lessons when I've finished up
    my work.

"I'm on my way through college, and I'm pay-
  ing for it here,
Some day I'll chuck this job and be a civil engineer.
I want an education, and the only way I had
Was to come and be a waiter, for I haven't any
  dad."

I don't know how to say it, but some day I know
  I'll hear,
If I still am with the living, of a civil engineer
Who has earned his way to glory, and I'll smile
  at his renown
And say: "There stands the waiter of that little
  college town."

A Man Must Want

It's wanting keeps us young and fit.
  It's wanting something just ahead
And striving hard to come to it,
  That brightens every road we tread.

That man is old before his time
  Who is supremely satisfied
And does not want some hill to climb
  Or something life has still denied.

The want of poverty is grim,
    It has a harsh and cruel sting,
But fill the cup up to the brim,
    And that's a far more hopeless thing.

A man must want from day to day,
    Must want to reach a distant goal
Or claim some treasure far away,
    For want's the builder of the soul.

He who has ceased to want has dropped
    The working tools of life and stands
Much like an old-time clock that's stopped
    While Time is mouldering his hands.

I'm truly sorry for the man,
    Though he be millionaire or king,
Who does not hold some cherished plan
    And says he does not want a thing.

Want is the spur that drives us on
    And oft its praises should be sung,
For man is old when want is gone —
    It's what we want that keeps us young.

Bill and Jim drove into town on a pleasant
    summer day,
Puffed their pipes and talked of things in a
    friendly sort of way,
Talked of crops and politics, neighbors and the
    price of nails,
Then, as they were jogging on, passed a fellow
    splitting rails.
" Who's that yonder, Bill? " says Jim, " I don't
    seem to know his face."
" That's Abe Lincoln," answered Bill — " got a
    shabby sort of place."

Lawsuit going on one day, Bill and Jim had
    time to spare,
Dropped into the court awhile, found most all
    their neighbors there.
" Moonlight night," one witness said — pris-
    oner's chances mighty small,
Till his lawyer rose and proved there wasn't any
    moon at all.
" Who's defending him? " says Jim, " rather
    clever, I should say."
" That's Abe Lincoln," answered Bill, " homely
    as a bale of hay."

Politics was getting hot, meetings almost every
      night,
Orators from north and south talking loudly for
      the right.
Bill and Jim were always there cheering for their
      party's cause,
Then one time a chap got up talking morals more
      than laws.
" Who's that speaking now? " says Jim, " think
      I've seen his face before."
" That's Abe Lincoln," answered Bill, " shall we
      go or hear some more? "

Moral of it isn't much, greatness may be round
      about,
But when seen from day to day men are slow to
      find it out.
Those who saw him splitting rails, those who
      heard him plead a case
Passed him by with little thought, laughing at
      his homely face.
Those who neighbored with the boy, those who
      saw his summer tan,
Those who lived in Lincoln's time never really
      knew the man.

The Mushroom Expert

Bill is a mushroom expert, and Bill is a friend
 of mine,
He has studied the amanita and all its ancestral
 line;
He goes to the fields each autumn to harvest a
 dinner treat
For he knows which are deadly fungi, and which
 are the ones to eat.

Bill can talk by the hour on mushrooms and he
 laughs at my timid fears,
He is still in the land of the living and has eaten
 the things for years;
He is wise in the lore of the meadow, the swamp
 and the dark ravine,
And I'd say, of the mushroom experts, he's the
 best that I've ever seen.

If ever I gathered mushrooms I'd carry them
 back to Bill
And ask him to look them over and pick out the
 ones that kill;
I'd trust to his certain knowledge and bank on
 his judgment, too,
For he is a shark on that stuff and can spiel it
 right off to you.

Bill knows 'em and loves 'em and eats 'em, and
    all through the days of fall
He's out with his little basket in search of the
    snowy ball;
And never I doubt his knowledge, I grant it sur-
    passes mine —
But during the mushroom season I don't go to
    Bill's to dine.

The Town of Used to Be

Used to think I'd like to go
To the town I used to know
As a little bare-foot lad,
Tanned of cheek an' always glad.
But it's been so long since I
Told the good old friends good-bye
An' set out for wealth an' fame,
That it cannot be the same,
An' maybe I'd better not
Spoil the picture that I've got.

Bill's been back, an' he tells me
Town's not what it used to be;
That old Barker's grocery store
Isn't open any more,
An' most folks we knew are gone,

Moved away or traveled on
To a brighter realm than this;
An' the girls we used to kiss
An' go courtin' with, somehow
Don't seem half so pretty now.

Folks have told me that the farm
Where I lived has lost its charm
An' they've paved the dusty street
Which was velvet to our feet,
An' it's now a thoroughfare
With the hum of motors there;
Wouldn't want to lose the joy
That I've treasured from a boy —
Guess I'd better keep always
Memories of those happier days.

I'm afraid of goin' back.
Memory still keeps the track
To those favorite haunts of mine
Like a painted canvas fine,
An' the old spots live with me
Just the way they used to be;
An' to see them now would seem
Much like shattering a dream,
So the town shall live with me
Just the way it used to be.

The Driver of the Truck

I envy him his care-free way, I envy him his
    smile,
The highway is his own domain, he rules it every
    mile;
The king who drives about by day, sends couriers
    on ahead
And buglers gay and soldiers brave, a path for
    him to spread;
But he may go his way alone nor fear that he'll
    be struck,
For monarch of the highway is the driver of the
    truck.

When I go driving down the road I must obey
    the rules,
I must watch out for all who come, the sane men
    and the fools,
And I must guard that car of mine with vigi-
    lance and care,
For even trifling accidents might strand me then
    and there;
But let who will bump into him, he's never out
    of luck,
No pleasure car can ever stop the driver of the
    truck.

He sits his seat in confidence, serene and quite
    content,
His heavy wheels are never dished, his axles
    never bent;
A locomotive engineer might jolt him from his
    place,
But nothing short of that would bring a tremor
    to his face.
He laughs his cheerful way along, too big for
    men to buck,
And even millionaires must dodge the driver of
    the truck.

Oh, kings and kaisers overthrown, who live in
    exile now,
And princes of the royal blood whose heads have
    had to bow
Before the people's mightier will, if you'd once
    more regain
The arrogance of happier days before they closed
    your reign,
You still can make the lowly flee and force the
    throngs to duck —
Just hustle out and get a job as driver of a truck.

The Radio

Since Pa put in the radio we have a lot of fun,
We hustle to my room upstairs as soon as sup-
     per's done
And Pa he tinkers with the discs to get it loud
     and clear,
Then says: "Wait just a minute now, there's
     nothing yet to hear.
Oh, now it's coming! Silence there! Now don't
     you move a thing.
Say Ma, this is a marvelous age — a lady's going
     to sing!"

Then Ma she listens for awhile, as pleased as
     she can be
And when I want to hear it, too, she says, " Don't
     bother me!
Your turn comes next and sister's, too; don't
     jump around that way,
I want to hear the orchestra — it's just begun
     to play.
I wish you children wouldn't fuss, I'm sure I
     cannot hear
While you are trying all the time to snatch it
     from my ear."

Then Pa takes up the thing awhile and says:
    " Oh, that's just great!
A man is telling stories now.   You kids will have
        to wait.
It's wonderful to think his voice is floating in
        the air
And people sitting in their homes can hear it
        everywhere —
All right, all right! It's your turn now.   Perhaps
        this man will teach
You youngsters how you should behave.   A par-
        son's going to preach."

Pa put that radio in for me — at least he told
        me so,
But if it's really mine or not, is something I don't
        know,
'Coz Pa he wants it all himself, to hear the
        funny things,
An' Ma must hear the concerts through when
        some great artist sings,
But when the parson starts to talk on Selfishness
        an' Sin,
Pa says: " Now it has come the time for you
        to listen in."

The Yellow Dog

It was a little yellow dog, a wistful thing to see,
A homely, skinny, battered pup, as dirty as could
be;
His ribs were showing through his hide, his
coat was thick with mud,
And yet the way he wagged his tail completely
captured Bud.

He had been kicked from door to door and
stoned upon his way,
"Begone!" was all he'd ever heard, 'twas all
that folks would say;
And yet this miserable cur, forever doomed to
roam,
Struck up a comradeship with Bud, who proudly
brought him home.

I've never seen so poor a dog in all my stretch
of years,
The burrs were thick upon his tail and thick
upon his ears;
He'd had to fight his way through life and carried many a scar,
But still Bud brought him home and cried: "Say,
can I keep him, Ma?"

I think the homeless terrier knows that age is
    harsh and stern,
And from the shabby things of life in scorn is
    quick to turn;
And when some scrubby yellow dog needs sym-
    pathy and joy,
He's certain of a friend in need, if he can find
    a boy.

The Fairy and the Robin

A fairy and a robin met
Beside a bed of mignonette.
The robin bowed and raised his hat,
And smiled a smile as wide as — that —
Then said: "Miss Fairy, I declare,
I'd kiss you, only I don't dare."

The fairy curtsied low and said:
"Your breast is such a lovely red,
And you are such a handsome thing,
And, oh, such pretty songs you sing --
I'd gladly kiss you now, but I
May only kiss a butterfly."

The robin spoke a silly word:
"I'm sorry I was born a bird!
Were I a fairy-man instead,

Then you and I might some day wed."
The fairy laughed and said: "My dear,
God had to have some robins here.

"Be glad you're what you are and sing
And cheer the people in the Spring.
I play with children as I'm told,
But you bring joy to young and old,
And it seems always strange to me
I'm one the old folks never see."

The robin spoke: "Perhaps it's best.
I'll sing my songs and show my breast
And be a robin, and you stay
And share in all the children's play.
God needs us both, so let us try
To do our duty — you and I."

How do I know they said these things?
I saw the robin spread his wings,
I saw the fairy standing up
Upon a golden buttercup,
I hid myself behind a wall
And listened close and heard it all.

Good Night

How many times we've said good night
   And kissed her as we turned away,
Knowing that with the morning light
   She'd greet the beauty of the day.

We left her sleeping in her bed
   And tiptoed gently from her room,
And when the soft " good night " was said,
   The parting brought no touch of gloom.

She would be there when we should rise,
   To greet us with her lovely smile —
The sunbeams dancing in her eyes,
   And night seemed such a little while.

Her spirit, till the break of day,
   Would leave this little world of ours
For brighter realms wherein to play,
   Where fairies danced among the flowers.

Sometimes we watched her as she dreamed
   And knew that she was free from care,
And always lovelier she seemed
   When morning found her smiling there.

" Good night, good night! sweet Marjorie! "
   We will be brave with you away.
Some glad to-morrow there shall be,
   We'll come to you at break of day.

The Man Who Gets Promoted

The ordinary fellow does an ordinary task,
    He's mighty fond of " good enough " and lets
        it go at that;
But the chap who gets promoted, or the raise he
        doesn't ask,
    Has just a little something more than hair
        beneath his hat.

The ordinary fellow lives an ordinary day,
    With the ordinary fellow he is anxious to be
        quit;
But the chap who draws attention and the larger
        weekly pay,
    Has a vision for the future and is working
        hard for it.

He tackles every problem with the will to see
        it through,
    He does a little thinking of the work that
        comes to hand;
His eyes are always open for the more that he
        can do,
    You never find him idle, merely waiting a
        command.

The ordinary fellow does precisely as he's told,
But someone has to tell him what to do, and
how, and when;
But the chap who gets promoted fills the job he
has to hold
With just a little something more than ordinary men.

The Lesson of the Crate

It seemed an unimportant task,
Too trifling for a chief to ask,
A little thing, nor could he see
The need to do it thoroughly;
He fancied none could ever tell
Whether he did it very well
Or slighted it, yet, truth to say,
On him depended much that day.

He was to nail a wooden crate,
No chance in that for splendor great,
No chance to prove his gift of skill,
A thankless post was his to fill;
Well nailed or not, 'twould be the same,
The world would never learn his name —
And yet that wooden crate was filled
With what had taken months to build.

He did not see or understand
Just what was passing 'neath his hand —
That as that wooden crate was nailed,
A plan succeeded or it failed;
That miles away men stood in wait
Depending on that simple crate,
For not a wheel could turn or drive
Until it safely should arrive.

He drove his nails, and let it go,
Thinking that none would ever know
Whose hand had held the hammer there
Or, knowing it, would ever care;
Yet in a few brief days there came
The news that burned his cheeks with
      shame:
" Broken in shipment and we stay
Facing another month's delay."

Vain is the skill of workmen great;
Unless the boy who makes the crate
Shall give his best to driving nails,
The work of all the others fails.
There is no unimportant task.
Whatever duty life may ask,
On it depends the greater plan —
There is no unimportant man!

Bill and I Went Fishing

Bill and I went fishing. Quit our beds at four,
Got a hasty breakfast and softly closed the door,
Packed the bait and tackle, pushed the boat away,
Took the oars and started — without a word to
     say.

Lake was smooth as crystal, sun was breaking
     through
With a blaze of glory — old, but always new;
Bill and I both watched it, grateful for the day,
Spellbound by the beauty — but not a word to
     say.

Threw the anchor over, started in to fish,
Heard the reels a-clicking, heard the wet lines
     swish,
Now and then we'd get one big enough to play,
Sport and plenty of it — but not a word to say.

Bill was busy dreaming, I was thinking, too,
Lazy-like and wondering what makes skies so
     blue;
Puffed our pipes in silence, let our minds just
     stray
'Round and 'round about us — but not a word
     to say.

Got back home that evening, happy as could be,
I was proud of William, he was proud of me,
Just the pal for fishing. Here's the common
        touch —
Said it of each other — " Never talks too much."

Easter

They found the great stone rolled away
    And Him whom men had crucified,
    With cruel spears had pierced His side
And mocked with jests and gibes that day,
    Gone from the darkness and the gloom
    Of Death's grim tomb.

Where He had slept in Death's embrace
    The linen of His shroud was piled,
    And white-robed angels gently smiled
And bade them walk into the place.
    " The Lord is risen! " to them they said,
    " He is not dead."

Keep ye the faith and still be brave!
    From every tomb that Easter day
    The stone of death was rolled away;
The soul lives on beyond the grave,
    Death is but rest from pain and strife —
    The gate to life!

October

October and the crimsoned trees,
The smell of smoke upon the breeze,
The morning mist and autumn's chill,
The brown of death upon the hill —
And yet, a sense of loveliness
Which pen or brush cannot express.

A strange, mysterious calm which seems
The canvas of a thousand dreams;
The calm of duty nobly done,
The peace of battles truly won,
The joy with which all hearts are thrilled,
A sense of promises fulfilled.

Beyond October winter waits
To pile its snow before the gates;
What men call death shall hurl its stroke
Alike at plant or giant oak —
And yet beneath the snowdrifts deep
We know the violets merely sleep.

Mankind has its October, too,
When little more there is to do,
And we may claim the sweet content
Of strength that has been nobly spent —
And yet we fear, when comes the snow,
There is no spring where we shall go.

October with its lovely breath
Voices the cry: there is no death!
Men read it in a thousand ways;
We see beyond the mist and haze
Which shroud the hills and valleys deep,
That all shall wake who fall asleep.

Mother and the Styles

Dresses high and dresses low,
Fashion bids them come and go;
Tresses bobbed and tresses long,
Fashion sways the moving throng;
What was new becomes the old,
Thus this changing life is told.
First we view it with a smile,
Then adopt the latest style—
But with all the passing days,
Mothers never change their ways.

Gay of heart and bright of face,
Fashion seems to rule the place.
With the swinging of the clock
Youth gives Age another shock,
Flaunting into public view
Something Age would never do,
Laughing at us when we preach,

Scornful of us when we teach—
But with all of fashion's wiles,
Mothers never change their styles.

Motherhood's no fickle thing,
To be changed each fall and spring;
As it was, so it remains,
Spite of all its cares and pains.
Joy may call and pleasure lure
But a mother's love is pure,
And the baby sinks to rest,
Pillowed on her lovely breast,
Closing little drowsy eyes
To the softest lullabies.

Mothers worry night and day
When their children are away;
Mothers grieve when they are ill,
Always have and always will.
They would shield you with their care
Every day and every where,
And they're happy through and through
At the slightest smile from you —
To the ending of their days
Mothers never change their ways.

High Chair Days

High chair days are the best of all,
  Or so they seem to me,
Days when tumbler and platter fall
  And the King smiles merrily;
When the regal arms and the regal feet
A constant patter of music beat,
And the grown-ups bow in a gracious way
To the high chair monarch who rules the day.

High chair days, and the throne not dressed
  In golden or purple hues
But an old style thing, let it be confessed,
  His grandmother used to use;
Its legs are scarred and a trifle bowed,
But the king who sits on the chair is proud,
And he throws his rattle and silver cup
For the joy of making us pick them up.

The old high chair in the dining room
  Is a handsomer thing by far
Than the costly chairs in the lonely gloom
  Of the childless mansions are,
For the sweetest laughter the world has known
Comes day by day from that humble throne,
And the happiest tables, morn and night,
Have a high chair placed at the mother's right.

The old high chair is a joy sublime,
　　Yet it brings us its hour of pain,
For we've put it away from time to time,
　　Perhaps never to need again;
Yet God was good, and the angles tapped,
And again was the old high chair unwrapped,
And proud was I when I heard the call
To bring it back to the dining hall.

There are griefs to meet and cares to face
　　Through the years that lie ahead;
The proudest monarch must lose his place
　　And lie with the splendid dead;
I know there are blows I shall have to meet,
I must pay with the bitter for all life's sweet,
But I live in dread of that coming day
When forever the high chair goes away.

Whooping Cough

There is a reason, I suppose, for everything
     which comes —
Why youngsters fall from apple trees and babies
     suck their thumbs;
And though I can't explain it all, when trouble
     comes I know
That since by Providence 'tis willed, it must be
     wiser so.
But knowing this, I still insist we'd all be better
     off
If little children could escape the dreaded whoop-
     ing cough.

I never see a red-faced child in spasms violent
But what I wonder why to babes such suffering
     is sent.
Though mumps and measles, chicken pox and
     scarlet fever, too,
Beset the lives of those I love, I still can see them
     through;
But terror seems to chill my blood the minute that
     I hear
That awful sign that someone's child with whoop-
     ing cough is near.

Old women say it has to be, but I grow pale as
    death
When I behold a boy or girl in anguish fight for
    breath.
They tell me not to be alarmed, but I'm not made
    of steel,
And every touch of agony the youngster has, I
    feel;
And could I run this world of ours, the first thing
    I'd cut off
From all the things which have to be, would be
    the whooping cough.

Over the Crib

Over the crib where the baby lies,
Countless beautiful visions rise
Which only the mothers and fathers see,
Visions of splendor that is to be,
Pictures of laughter and joy and song
As the years come sweeping us all along.
Care seldom startles the happy eyes
Over the crib where the baby lies.

A wonderful baby lying there!
And strangers smile at the happy pair,
Proud and boastful, for all they see
Is the dimpled chin and the dimpled knee;

But never a little one comes to earth
That isn't a wonderful babe at birth,
And never a mother who doesn't see
Glorious visions of joy to be.

Over the crib where the baby lies,
Dreams of splendor and pride arise,
Deeds of valor and deeds of love
Hover about and shine above
The tiny form, and the future glows
With a thousand dreams which the mother
    knows,
And beauty dances before her eyes
Over the crib where the baby lies.

Yet we smile at her and we smile at him,
For we are old and our eyes are dim
And we have forgotten and don't recall
Yet world-wide over the mothers dream
The visions we saw when our babes were
    small,
And ever they see in a golden stream,
Wonderful joys in the by-and-by
Over the cribs where their babies lie.

Grass and Children

I used to want a lovely lawn, a level patch of
    green,
For I have marveled many times at those that I
    have seen,
And in my early dreams of youth the home that
    I should keep
Possessed a lawn of beauty rare, a velvet carpet
    deep,
But I have changed my mind since then — for
    then I didn't know
That where the feet of children run the grass
    can never grow.

Now I might own a lovely lawn, but I should
    have to say
To all the little ones about, " Go somewhere else
    to play!"
And I should have to stretch a wire about my
    garden space
And make the home where gladness reigns, a
    most forbidding place.
By stopping all the merriment which now is ours
    to know,
In time, beyond the slightest doubt, the tender
    grass would grow.

But oh, I want the children near, and so I never
    say,
When they are romping around the home, " Go
    somewhere else to play!"
And though my lawn seems poorly kept, and
    many a spot is bare,
I'd rather see, than growing grass, the youngsters
    happy there.
I've put aside the dream I had in that far long
    ago —
I'd rather have a playground than a place for
    grass to grow.

The Hills of Faith

The hills are in the mist to-day,
Their purple robes are put away.
Like coast guards in their yellow coats
    They face the driving rain;
Like coast guards in their yellow coats,
Who watch the sea for ship-wrecked boats,
They watch the land for human craft
    In trouble on the plain.

The gray clouds rush among their peaks,
Some weakness there the storm-king seeks.
A frightened boulder breaks away
    And rolls into the glen;

A tree is crushed to earth again,
But staunch and brave the hills remain,
A symbol of unfaltering faith
    To all the hosts of men.

Time was the hills were tinged with gold,
About them seas of crimson rolled,
A gentle beauty graced their brows
    As delicate as May
Who comes with blossoms in her hair.
They laughed away the summer there,
But now sublimely stern they stand,
    Attired in somber gray.

Symbols of strength, unmoved they keep
Their place against the winds that sweep;
Defenders of our coast of faith,
    They signal to us all
That what is strong and best and true
Shall breast the gale and live it through
To greet the birth of spring again
    And hear the song bird's call.

Last Night the Baby Cried

Last night the baby cried. And I,
    Roused from a sound and soothing sleep,
Wondered to hear that little cry.
    For ten long years in slumber deep
I've lived my nights, and so it seemed
That what I'd heard I'd only dreamed.

For ten long years a banging gate,
    The milkman's whistle, or the horn
Of motors driven at rapid rate,
    Have wakened me at early dawn;
But late last night awake was I,
Thinking I'd heard a baby cry.

I leaned upon my elbow there
    And wondered did I dream or not?
But once again upon the air
    The call came from her tiny cot!
Then peacefully I turned and smiled
To hear the crying of our child.

Lonely and still the house has seemed
    For ten long years, but once again
We have the joy of which we'd dreamed —
    The joy which many seek in vain!
Oh, happy, happy home, thought I,
That wakes to hear a baby cry.

The True Critic

There is one critic which a man should heed
    And strive with all his strength to satisfy;
Whether it be in big or little deed,
    One sits in judgment with a watchful eye.

One voice there is which flatters not for gain
    Nor censures honest effort as a pose,
One voice which never speaks to cause us pain,
    Nor seeks to tell the world how much it knows.

Yet if it tell us we have done our best,
    Have kept the faith and labored to be true,
We can lie down at night in peace to rest
    Nor mind what others say or think or do.

If but this eye which reads our inmost thought
    See no dishonor in the stand we take,
If but this voice can praise the fight we've fought,
    We need not heed the storm that critics make.

If we but live with Conscience as our guide,
    We rob the colder critics of their sting;
If but that voice of us can speak in pride,
    We need not heed the barbs which others fling.

If it can say we've truly done our best,
    And call our motives worthy, though we fail,
We then can turn our faces to the west,
    Scorning the lesser critics who assail.

A Song in Everything

There is a song in everything,
   In every little care that comes,
   In babies as they suck their thumbs,
The tunes the brave canaries sing,
   The mother's patient, gentle smile,
   The glory of the after-while.

There is no sadness but is sweet
   With fragrance, and there is no day
   But spreads some beauty on life's way;
The dusty and the weary feet
   Upon their homeward journey bring
   Delights which loving hearts may sing.

The high chair and the cradle, too,
   Have ever set brave lips to song;
   No grief has ever lived so long
But turned to music as it grew,
   And every hour of strife and pain
   Leaves in the heart some sweet refrain.

Lord, teach me this, from day to day,
   To find beyond the hurt and care
   Thy mercy shining everywhere;
Let me rejoice that children play,
   And know when bitter tempests sting
   There is a song in everything

Triumph

Back of every golden dream,
Every engine hissing steam,
Back of every hammer falling
And of every deed men dare;
Back of every tilt and fight
Is the coming home at night
To the loved ones who are waiting
In the victory to share.

When all is said and done
And the battle's lost or won,
It's the laughter of the children
And the mother's gentle smile,
It's the pride of those you know,
Good old friends who love you so,
That make the prize worth having
And the victory worth while.

'Tis not in success alone
That achievement's worth is known.
If we had no friends to cheer us
And no one at home to care;
If man's glory as a fighter
Did not make a few eyes brighter
He would cease to try for conquest
And would never do or dare.

Back of every man you'll find
Loving hearts who stay behind,
Watching, waiting, patient, loyal,
As he strives to meet the test,
And the thought which drives him daily
Is that they shall meet him gayly,
And shall glory in his triumph
On the day he does his best.

Ships

To-day, if I were free, I think
I'd wander to the river's brink
And watch the great ships steaming by —
The stream below, above the sky —
And see those vessels bearing then
The countless hopes of mortal men.

And I could lie upon the shore
And glimpse the mother at the door
Watching and waiting, every trip,
To see the coming of the ship,
For that great hull which carries grain
Also brings home her boy again.

I wonder if the wheelsman knows,
As he the guiding rudder throws,
How many hopes and dreams and fears
Are burdened in the ship he steers?
Depending on his watchful eyes
The laughter of a lifetime lies.

Men write his cargo down as ore,
Or grain or coal, but it is more —
It's women's smiles and women's tears
And little children's happy years,
For human destines await
The safe arrival of his freight.

We are but smaller packet ships
Set out upon our various trips,
Chartered for gold, or skill or fame,
Listed and registered by name,
Yet burdened with the smiles and tears
Our own must know throughout the years.

The women and the children wait
For us each evening at the gate,
Glad when we safely come from town
And desolate if we go down.
Bitter their years if we shall fail
To hold the course and breast the gale.

Mother's Way

Tender, gentle, brave and true,
Loving us whate'er we do!
Waiting, watching at the gate
For the footsteps that are late,
Sleepless through the hours of night
Till she knows that we're all right;
Pleased with every word we say —
That is every mother's way.

Others sneer and turn aside.
Mother welcomes us with pride;
Over-boastful of us, too,
Glorying in all we do,

First to praise and last to blame,
Love that always stays the same,
Following us where'er we stray —
That is every mother's way.

She would grant us all we seek,
Give her strength where we are weak.
Beauty? She would let it go
For the joy we yearn to know.
Life? She'd give it gladly, too,
For the dream that we pursue;
She would toil that we might play —
That is every mother's way.

Not enough for her are flowers —
Her life is so blent with ours
That in all we dare and do
She is partner, through and through;
Suffering when we suffer pain,
Happy when we smile again,
Living with us, night and day —
That is every mother's way.

Life Needs Us All

There is so much that we can do —
   A kind word spoken here and there
   Will ease another's weight of care;
Life needs us all. The splendid few
   Who rise to fame, with all their skill
   Your post and mine can never fill.

If we who have not wealth or fame
   Should fail in all our little deeds,
   The world would sink beneath its needs.
Not by the greatness of a name,
   Nor by the splendor of success,
   Are hearts restored to happiness.

About us all are those who need
   The gifts which we have power to give;
   We can be friendly while we live
And by some thoughtful, kindly deed,
   Can help another on his way —
   And that is service, come what may.

What though we miss the heights of skill,
   The splendor of the greater few,
   There is so much that we can do;
There is a place which we can fill —
   Always about us while we live
   Are those who need what we can give.

A Certain Man

I cherish the picture of a man
  Who has not been, but is to be.
His cheek is bronzed by the summer tan
  And his smile is fair to see.
His word is good and his heart is true
And he loves the old red, white and blue.

I vision him oft, and where'er he goes
  Glad voices give him a warm hello.
The trust of the little ones he knows
  And respect of friend or foe —
For never the scarlet mark of shame
Has marred his record or touched his name.

He walks the world in a kindly way.
  He laughs when the jest is fair.
The wide outdoors is his field of play
  And he loves the beauties there.
He hears God's word in the whispering trees
And the song of birds and the drone of bees.

I talk to him oft when the night is still,
  I think of him day by day;
He hasn't arrived, but I pray he will
  When his youth has passed away.
And what is his name and who is he?
The man that I hope my son will be.

What a Father Wants to Know

You would take my girl away!
What is there that I can say
Save the things all fathers think,
Seldom put in printer's ink?
Little care I for your fame,
Or the glory you may claim,
Or the fortune you may earn;
These are not my deep concern —
This I really want to know,
Will you always love her so?

It is fine enough to tell
That to-day you're doing well;
I appreciate your skill
And I think some day you will
Climb the ladder of success
To your lasting happiness;
But if all this should be had
And my little girl be sad,
I'd regret my whole life through
Having given her to you.

Will you always love her so?
That is what I want to know.
Will you comfort her and stay
At her side from day to day?
Knowing she must bear your name,

Will you shield her from all shame?
This the burden on my mind,
Will you thoughtful be and kind?
All that matters is to know
That you'll always love her so.

The Luckless Fisherman

They laughed when I came home last night
And said I didn't get a bite;
They snickered an' they joked at me,
And all the fellows asked to see
The ones I'd caught, "Oho!" said they,
"He's been out fishing all this day
An' hasn't caught a single thing,
He never got a fish to string."

They laughed at me, but all their jeers
Traveled no further than my ears.
'Twas true I'd fished all day without
Snaring a single speckled trout,
But what of that? I'd had a day
That I could loaf and dream away,
I'd chummed with birds and friendly trees
And been as care-free as the breeze.

I'd rested wheresoe'er I'd willed,
To me the hum of trade was stilled,
I'd let my thoughts go wandering far
To where life's happier glories are;
I'd whistled like a boy once more,
And even stretched full length on shore
To watch the white clouds sail the blue,
The very way I used to do.

They laughed when I came home at night
And said I didn't get a bite.
They seemed to think my luck was bad.
They couldn't guess the fun I'd had
And couldn't know that all that day
I'd been a free man, blithe and gay,
And though of fish I'd landed none,
I'd caught the joys for which I'd gone.

Consolation

"It is all for the best," so they said
As I stood by my dead.
But I doubted the word
That so often I heard;
I could catch but the moan
Of the mother, alone,
And feel but the blow
Which had stricken us so.

"Why," I cried, "should it be
God must so punish me?
Why should my baby die
When are hundreds near by,
Old and feeble of breath,
Waiting only for death?"
And they answered me low:
"God has ordered it so."

But to-day, through the years
That have ended our tears,
We have memories rare
That no others may share;
We can look back and see
Why the blow had to be —
By that mound and its sod,
We are closer to God.

If It's Worth While

If it's worth while, then it's worth a few blows,
  Worth a few setbacks and worth a few bruises;
If it's worth while — and it is, I suppose —
  It's worth keeping on, though the first strug-
    gle loses.

If it's worth while, then it's worth a good fight,
  Worth a few bouts with the demon, Disaster,
Worth going after with courage and might,
  Worth keeping on till you've proved you are
    master.

If it's worth while, then it's worth a few pains,
  Worth a few heartaches and worth a few sor-
    rows,
Worth clinging fast to the hope that remains,
  Worth going on through the doubtful to-mor-
    rows.

Stand to the battle and see the test through,
  Pay all you have in endurance and might for
    it;
If it's worth while and a good thing to do,
  Then it is worth all it costs in the fight for it.

The Letter

The postman whistled down the street
And seemed to walk on lighter feet,
And as he stepped inside her gate
He knew he carried precious freight;
He knew that day he carried joy —
He had the letter from her boy.

Day after day he'd kept his pace
And seen her careworn, gentle face.
She watched for him to come and took
The papers with an anxious look,
But disappointment followed hope—
She missed the one glad envelope.

He stopped to chat with her awhile
And saw the sadness of her smile,
He fancied he could hear her sigh
The morning that he traveled by;
He knew that when to-morrow came
She would be waiting just the same.

The boy who was so far away
Could never hear her gently say:
"Well, have you brought good news to me?"

Her eager face he could not see,
Or note the lines of anxious care
As every day she waited there.

But when he wrote, on lighter feet
The happy postman walked the street.
" Well, here it is, at last," he'd shout,
" To end the worry and the doubt."
The robin on the maple limb
Began to sing: " She's heard from him."

Her eyes with joy began to glow,
The neighbors round her seemed to know
That with the postman at the door
Sweet peace had come to her once more.
When letters bring so much delight,
Why do the sons forget to write?

The Tower Clock

Day after day the clock in the tower
Strikes on its resonant bell, the hour.
Telling the throngs in the city block
Once again it's ten o'clock!
Day after day, and the crowds pass on,
Till they and another hour have gone.

I heard it first as an eager lad,
The largest clock which the city had,

And it rang the hour in the self-same way
That it rings it out for the town to-day,
And many who heard it then have gone,
Gone like the days that have journeyed on.

Mighty and many the throngs have grown,
Many the changes the town has known,
But the old clock still in its tower stands,
Telling the hour with its silent hands;
And the great pass by and they come no more,
But the bell still rings as it did of yore.

And I think to-day as I hear it ring
That the fame men crave is a fleeting thing.
Unchanged, unswayed by the pomps men praise,
The old clock high in its tower stays,
Sounding the hours for the great and low
As it sounded them in the long ago.

So when the throngs that are here pass by
And the pride of to-day in the dust shall lie,
When the new crowds come in their search for
        power,
The self-same clock in the self-same tower
Shall still ring out in the city block,
For them, as for us, it is ten o'clock.

The Busy Summer Cottage

Our friends have automobiles now. The sum-
    mer cottage where we went
To rest beside the water's blue in peace and in-
    dolent content
Is but an hour's swift ride away. So bright and
    early Sunday morn
Before the breakfast eggs are cooked, we hear
    the honking of the horn.

We must have bathing suits for ten, although
    our family numbers four;
Beds must be made for all who come, though
    father sleeps upon the floor;
Dishes and knives and forks and spoons are
    gathered in one huge display,
For we must be prepared to feed the visitors
    who come our way.

From Friday noon till Monday morn full many
    a weary trip I take,
Rowing the women and their babes upon the
    bosom of the lake;
And by that law which rules a host I'm at the
    mercy of the crew,
I must, until they say good-bye, do everything
    they wish to do.

The chef in yonder large hotel is not a busier
    man than I,
The fish for fifteen hungry mouths it is my duty
    now to fry,
And thus my glad vacation time from dawn to
    dusk is filled with chores,
For friends have made our resting spot the bus-
    iest place in all outdoors.

Good Enough

My son, beware of " good enough,"
It isn't made of sterling stuff;
It's something any man can do,
It marks the many from the few,
It has no merit to the eye,
It's something any man can buy,
Its name is but a sham and bluff,
For it is never " good enough."

With " good enough " the shirkers stop
In every factory and shop;
With " good enough " the failures rest
And lose to men who give their best;
With " good enough " the car breaks down
And men fall short of high renown.
My son, remember and be wise,
In " good enough " disaster lies.

With " good enough " have ships been wrecked,
The forward march of armies checked,
Great buildings burned and fortunes lost;
Nor can the world compute the cost
In life and money it has paid
Because at " good enough " men stayed.
Who stops at " good enough " shall find
Success has left him far behind.

There is no " good enough " that's short
Of what you can do and you ought.
The flaw which may escape the eye
And temporarily get by,
Shall weaken underneath the strain
And wreck the ship or car or train,
For this is true of men and stuff —
Only the best is " good enough."

I would not, if I could, recall some customs that
    are gone.
I'm glad that wreath of immortelles I need not
    look upon —
That cold, imperishable thing of wax, in colors
    gay,
Which hung upon the parlor wall in Grandma's
    earlier day,
No longer shrieks its warning grim that mortal
    life must cease —
And yet I'm sorry we have lost the old-time
    chimney piece.

The modern mantel, I admit, is striking to the
    eye,
And yet it lacks the wealth of charm we knew
    in days gone by;
For on the little marble shelf above the grate
    fire's glow
Were all the sacred treasures of the homestead
    in a row,
The pictures and the onyx clock, the globe of
    native birds,
Which told the things we loved the most in
    clearer speech than words.

There Mother kept in tenderness the trinkets of
the years,
The tokens of her happier days, the symbols of
her tears;
The glossy cabinet photographs, the candlesticks
of brass,
The picture of Niagara Falls blown into heavy
glass,
And there above the grate fire's glow, for every
eye to see,
Were all the sacred treasures from her book of
memory.

But Time has swept these things away, the mantel now is bare.
The attic dust lies thick upon the joys once
valued there;
The photographs are stored away, the birds long
since have flown,
Nor is it now good form to show the treasured
things we own,
For when the newer customs come, the ones of
old must cease,
And yet I'm sorry that we had to lose the chim-
ney piece.

The Crocus

A yellow crocus bloomed today.
  Where all is dead and bleak and bare,
It flashed its light along the way
  And radiantly twinkled there.

Out of the darkness and the gloom,
  Braving the blizzard's bitter sting,
There came this golden bit of bloom
  To herald the advancing spring.

"Hold out! Hold out!" it seemed to say,
  "Soon must the siege of winter fall,
The daffodils are on their way,
  The hyacinths have heard you call.

"Behind me comes a countless throng
  Of bigger, braver blooms than I;
The woods shall shortly ring with song,
  Spring's glorious army draweth nigh."

A yellow crocus flashed today
  Its torch of faith for all to see —
The troops of spring are on the way,
  The captive earth will soon be free.

My Goals

A little braver when the skies are gray,
    A little stronger when the road seems long,
A little more of patience through the day,
    And not so quick to magnify a wrong.

A little kinder, both of thought and deed,
    A little gentler with the old and weak,
Swifter to sense another's pressing need,
    And not so fast the hurtful phrase to speak.

These are my goals — not flung beyond my
        power,
    Not dreams of glory, beautiful but vain,
Not the great heights where buds of genius
        flower,
    But simple splendors which I ought to gain.

These I can do and be from day to day
    Along the humble pathway where I plod,
So that at last when I am called away
    I need not make apologies to God.

The Carpet on the Stairs

Let others sing in modern ways, it's joy enough
    for me
To sing in good old-fashioned rhyme the days
    that used to be.
The page of boyhood's scribbled full with things
    we used to do,
The fun we had, the games we played, the little
    tasks we knew,
And back to mind there comes today the hard-
    est of our cares,
That springtime job of putting down the carpet
    on the stairs.

Housecleaning time meant weary legs and hands
    and aching backs,
For no more tedious job there is than driving
    carpet tacks.
Then mother told us what to do, and on our
    hands and knees
We stretched and hauled and pulled and tugged
    and did our best to please;
But, oh! I well remember now one task which
    patience wears,
That awkward, muscle straining job of carpeting
    the stairs.

We'd start upon the topmost step and let the
    carpet roll,
But then began a feat of strength to try the
    bravest soul.
The corners must be folded so and stretched and
    firmly tacked,
With mother watching every move as down the
    stairs we backed;
And many a time we've reached the end, dis-
    covering there and then
It wouldn't do at all that way and must be laid
    again.

No more we break our finger nails and set our
    knees on fire
In stretching carpets on the floors, no more our
    muscles tire;
No more the mother stands above our bended
    forms to see
That every tack is driven home the way it ought
    to be.
The times are very different now, and no one
    ever shares
The joy and pain of long ago, while carpeting
    the stairs.

Horse and Cutter Days

Winters are not what they used to be in the
    cities of haste and rush;
The snow is white for a little while, then turns
    to an ugly slush.
And the rapid wheels of the motor cars grind
    all of its beauty down —
But I long for the horse and cutter days we
    knew in the little town.

Then the world stayed white for a month or two
    and the snow drifts higher grew
And cheeks were pink with the glow of health
    and the joys we youngsters knew,
Then sleigh bells added a merry lilt to the cold
    and crispy air
And youth and maid in an open sleigh were
    always a happy pair.

We hitched a ride to the runners strong and
    the snow flew from our feet,
But it's dangerous now to hitch a ride on the
    dark and crowded street,
And the raucous honk of the motor horn has
    banished the sleigh bell's song,
For winter days are cheerless now and winter
    nights are long.

Perhaps it's well that our customs change and
      good that we travel on,
But blent with the smiles of our newer joys are
      sighs for the pleasures gone,
And I sometimes long for the drifted snow and
      the white and frosty ways,
For the cheeks of pink and the laughter gay of
      our horse and cutter days.

The Old-Time Lilac Bush

A lilac bush is a lovely thing
Wherever it blossoms in early spring,
But I have a tenderer regard
For the old-time bush in an old-time yard,
With the house near-by and the youngsters flown,
And the old folks living there all alone,
For always I fancy I can see
The visions that cling to the lilac tree.

The house still stands, but the walls are still,
And the storms have battered each window sill;
There's a tired, worn look on the humble place,
Like the weary look on the mother's face,
Yet somehow or other I seem to know
That joy reigned here in the long ago,
And somehow or other I seem to see
The dreams which cling to the lilac tree.

Time was those feeble hands were strong
And the faltering footsteps danced along;
Time was youth romped in that lonely place,
But never the years will halt their pace,
And the young must go, but the old will cling
To the home they've loved to the final Spring,
For they hear the laughter that used to be,
When the bloom comes back to the lilac tree.

A lilac bush is a lovely thing
Wherever it blossoms in early spring,
But, bent with age and the smiles and tears
Which come to all with the passing years,
It seems to me that it wears the glow
Of the golden days of the long ago,
For all that remains of the youth long gone
Is the lilac tree still blossoming on.

A Boy's Feet

I got a cowlick, an' it stands
Up straight, an' I got dirty hands,
An' if it shows a single speck
I have to go an' wash my neck,
An' every day Ma squints an' peers
To see if I have washed my ears;
But I ain't ever really neat
All on account of havin' feet.

These feet of mine are always wrong,
I mustn't shuffle 'em along
Or kick a stone that's in the way,
Or if I do someone will say:
"I wish you'd lift your feet a bit;
The way you walk gives me a fit!
Those shoes were new a week ago
An' now you've busted out the toe."

They're always peckin' at me, too,
For standin' like the fellers do.
An' just because my toes turn in,
The teacher makes the pupils grin
By tellin' me ten times a day:
"Please turn your toes the other way!"
An' even when I'm in my seat
She kicks if I just swing my feet.

If I get nervous an' I put
One shoe upon the other foot,
Or scrape the floor, they say: "My land!
Is that the way a boy should stand?"
An' if I rest 'em on a chair,
Ma says: "Don't put your feet up there!"
An' if I sit on them they roar:
"Please put your feet upon the floor!"

I'm gettin' tired of all this talk
About the way I stand or walk,
An' anyhow it seems to me,
At least as far as I can see,
My feet aren't any different than
The other fellers 'round here, an'
Some day my temper will explode —
It ain't my fault I'm pigeon-toed.

Old-Fashioned Remedies

Taking medicine to-day isn't what it used to be.
Castor oil is castor oil, but they've banished
    senna tea,
And they've sugar coated now all the bitter
    things we took,
Mother used to brew for us from the family
    doctor book.
Now I tell that boy of mine when he starts to
    make a fuss,
He is lucky not to be taking what they gave to
    us.

Seems the kitchen stove back then always had
    a pan or two
Brewing up a remedy for the ailments which
    we knew,
Something mother said we'd need surely in a little
    while,
Senna tea for stomach ills and its brother,
    camomile;
But I vow the worst of all remedies they gave
    to me
Was that gummy, sticky stuff known and served
    as flaxseed tea.

Boy, put down that little pill, take your powders
    and be glad
You're not getting what they gave when your
    father was a lad.
Mother's hand was gentle, but rough and hard
    it seemed to be
When she sat beside my bed rubbing goose-
    grease into me.
Getting well is easy now. Take your medicine
    and smile,
You are lucky that it's not senna tea or camo-
    mile.

The Tumbler at the Sink

The houses of the rich folks are very fine to see,
But after all I fancy they'd never do for me —
For a butler guards the doorway, and a staff of
    servants wait
To gratify your slightest wish, like messengers
    of state.
They're there to do your bidding, and should
    you want a drink
They'll never let you get it from the tumbler at
    the sink.

Now it may be I'm old fashioned, but to really
feel at home,
I like to be permitted all around the house to
roam,
And I like to find the kitchen, with the towel
upon the door,
And the gayly colored picture from the corner
grocery store.
There's a comfortable feeling which the great
folks miss, I think,
In drinking, when you're thirsty, from the tumbler at the sink.

There's a charm about the kitchen which no
other room can boast,
And when you think about it, it's the one we
need the most.
It is there we find her smiling when we come
back home at night,
There the children dance about her as they're
pleading for a bite,
And it's there that eyes are brightest, cheeks the
pinkest of the pink,
And it's there, for all the thirsty, there's the
tumbler at the sink.

The Garden Catalogue

There's never frost nor blight nor weeds,
  Nor neighbor's chickens, cats or dogs,
To ruin all the tender seeds
  That flourish in the catalogues;
The humblest vine that's planted there
Blossoms without the slightest care.

There are no withered stalks to see,
  No pitiful attempts to thrive,
No shrub that struggles desperately
  To catch the sun and stay alive.
In catalogues the larkspur seems
To match the gardener's fondest dreams.

The red geranium is strong,
  Its clump of blossom full and round,
No windstorm ever comes along
  To sweep the cosmos to the ground,
No youngster ever bats a ball
Among the roses, straight and tall.

I turn the pages o'er and o'er
  And see the pansies dark as wine,
And think, as I have thought before,
  These are superior to mine;
In my poor garden, never yet
Has bloomed such lovely mignonette.

Since pansies have the storms to face
    And men must battle day by day,
They cannot wear the charm and grace
    Their printed catalogues display;
Life is much sterner than it looks
And scars are seldom shown in books.

Here on the Earth

Here is where the blows are struck,
    Here is where the wrong is done,
Here are toilers in the muck;
    Here beneath the shining sun,
Pain and hurt and sin abide,
Here is where our souls are tried.

What's beyond I cannot say,
    Save my faith that all is well;
There the wrongs are cast away,
    There in peace the angels dwell,
But this life on earth and sea
Holds so much that need not be.

I would not remain afar
    Thinking only of my soul;
Here where hungry children are,
    Here where hatred mars the scroll,
Thought and time and strength I'd give
Bettering this life we live.

Not to-morrow, but to-day,
　　I would serve another's need,
I would smooth another's way,
　　Bind the cruel wounds that bleed;
Death will soothe the weary brow,
But my hand would smooth it now.

Life has need of kindly men,
　　Just, courageous, true and brave,
But that need is ended when
　　Comes the sexton to the grave;
Let me, then, my duty face,
Making earth a happier place.

Let me serve the living here,
　　Not the dead across the bar,
Let me carry hope and cheer
　　Where the sad and hopeless are;
Angels wait upon the dead —
Let me smooth the path men tread.

I Mustn't Forget

I mustn't forget that I'm gettin' old —
    That's the worst thing ever a man can do.
I must keep in mind without bein' told
    That old ideas must give way to new.
Let me be always upon my guard
    Never a crabby old man to be,
Youth is too precious to have it marred
    By the cranky whims of a man like me.

I must remember that customs change
    An' I've had my youth an' my hair is gray,
Mustn't be too surprised at strange
    Or startlin' things that the youngsters say;
Mustn't keep the bit in their mouths too tight,
    Which is something old people are apt to do.
What used to be wrong may to-day be right
    An' it may not be wrong just becoz it's new.

Want 'em to like me an' want 'em to know
    That I need their laughter an' mirth an' song,
An' I want 'em near, 'coz I love 'em so,
    An' home is the place where their smiles be-
      long.
They're growin' up, an' it seems so queer
    To hear them talk of the views they hold,
But age with youth shouldn't interfere
    An' I mustn't forget that I'm gettin' old.

Old-Fashioned Dinners

It wasn't too much work for her in the days of
     long ago
To get a dinner ready for a dozen friends or so;
The mother never grumbled at the cooking she
     must do
Or the dusting or the sweeping, but she seemed
     to smile it through,
And the times that we were happiest, beyond
     the slightest doubt,
Were when good friends were coming and we
     stretched the table out.

We never thought, when we were young, to take
     our friends away
And entertain them at a club or in some swell
     cafe;
When mother gave a dinner, she would plan it
     all herself
And feed the people that she liked, the best things
     on the shelf.
Then one job always fell to me, for I was young
     and stout,
I brought the leaves to father when he stretched
     the table out.

That good old-fashioned table. I can see it still
     to-day
With its curious legs of varnished oak round
     which I used to play;
It wasn't much to look at, not as stylish or re-
     fined
Or as costly or as splendid as the oval, modern
     kind,
But it always had a welcome for our friends to
     sit about,
And though twenty guests were coming, we could
     always stretch it out.

I learned it from my mother — it is foolish
     pride to roam,
The only place to entertain your friends is right
     at home.
Just let them in by dozens, let them laugh and
     sing and play
And come to love and know them in the good
     old-fashioned way;
Home's the place for fun and friendship, home's
     the place where joy may shout,
And if you crowd our dining room, we'll stretch
     the table out.

The road lay straight before him, but the by-
    paths smiled at him
And the scarlet poppies called him to the forests
    cool and dim,
And the song birds' happy chorus seemed to lure
    him further on;
'Twas a day of wondrous pleasure — but the day
    was quickly gone.

He could not resist the laughter and the purling
    of a brook
Any more than gray old sages can resist some
    dusty book,
And though stern-faced duty bade him march
    the highway straight ahead,
" The trees are better company than busy men,"
    he said.

We wondered at his dreaming and his wander-
    ings far astray,
But we were counting values by the gold and
    silver way,
And sometimes as I saw him gazing idly at the
    sky,
I fancied he had pleasures of a sort I couldn't
    buy.

I fancy he saw something in the clouds above the
    trees
Which the gold and glory seeker passes by and
    never sees,
And I think he gathered something from the
    woods and running streams
Which is just as good as money to the man of
    many dreams.

Hot Mince Pie

I stood upon the coping of the tallest building
    known
And tried to walk that dangerous ledge, bare-
    footed and alone.
I started very bravely, then I turned to look be-
    hind
And saw a demon coming of the most ferocious
    kind;
He bade me get a move on, and I started in to
    run
And I slipped and lost my balance, and I knew
    that I was done.

I had a wild encounter with a mad and awful
    beast,
His eyes were bulged with malice, for he'd
    picked me for a feast.

I tried to scream, but couldn't. Then he growled
    a fearful note
And gave one spring towards me and his fangs
    sank in my throat,
One gulp and it was over — it was much too
    black to see,
But I knew beyond all question that the end
    had come for me.

I tumbled from an aeroplane and looped and
    looped around,
And was twenty-seven minutes on my journey
    to the ground;
I bumped a dozen steeples on my perilous descent
And left as many flagstaffs either snapped in two
    or bent —
But when I woke, in terror, I discovered with
    a sigh
How much of real excitement lurks in mother's
    hot mince pie.

The Laughing Boy

Always seeing the funny side,
  That's the glorious way of him.
Rollin' his head, with his mouth stretched wide,
  As quick to laugh as a duck to swim;
Whatever you say or whatever you do,
He'll answer you back with a chuckle or two.

Laughing from mornin' till night, it seems,
  Just chock full of the gift o' fun,
An' the angels send him their comic dreams
  So's he can grin for 'em every one,
An' his grandma says when he laughs her down,
He's the disrespectfullest boy in town.

Laughed at the prayer that the preacher spoke
  The night Ma asked him to come for tea;
Seemed to think it was all a joke,
  An' he actually winked his eye at me.
His ears are keen an' his mind is quick
An' his grin is ready for every trick.

" What'll we do? " says Ma to me,
  " With a boy like that who won't behave? "
An' I answer back: " We'll let him be.
  Old folks' faces are far too grave,
An' it's good for us all to have the joy
An' the rollickin' mirth of a laughin' boy."

Apples Ripe for Eating

Apples ripe for eating, and the grate fire blazing
   high,
And outside the moon of autumn fairly swim-
   ming in the sky;
The cellar packed with good things from the vine
   and field and tree —
Oh, the speech of man can't tell it, but it somehow seems to me
With such warmth and cheer around us, we
   should all burst into song
And store enough of gladness now to last our
   whole lives long.

Apples ripe for eating — there's a joy beyond
   compare
To pay for all our trouble and the burdens we
   must bear!
The bowl upon the table filled with round and
   rosy cheeks,
And enough down in the cellar to last all the
   winter weeks,
So that when the bowl is empty we can fill it
   up again —
And in spite of that we grumble and we bitterly
   complain.

I sometimes sit and wonder as we pack life's
      fruits away
And hoard them in the cellar for the bleak and
      wintry day,
Why the mind of man has never tried to store a
      stock of cheer
In the cellar of his memory for the barren time
      of year,
So that when joy's bowl is emptied and he thinks
      that life is vain,
He can seek his hoard of pleasures and just fill
      it up again.

Apples ripe for eating and a stock of them below
For the long cold nights of winter we shall
      shortly come to know,
So that when we need a pleasure that will seem
      to soothe the soul
We can wander to the cellar and fill up the apple
      bowl;
So we could, if we were mindful, when our
      hearts with grief are sad.
Refresh our faltering courage with the pleasures
      we have had.

When There's Company for Tea

When there's company for tea
Things go mighty hard with me;
Got to sit an' wait an' wait
Till the last guest's cleaned his plate,
An' I mustn't ask Ma what
Kind of pie it is she's got,
Mustn't crunch my napkin up
Or dip cookies in my cup.

When there's company for tea
Home don't seem like home to me;
Got to wash my ears an' neck
Till they do not show a speck;
Got to brush my hair an' then
Got to change my waist again,
Then walk slowly down stairs an'
Try to be a gentleman.

When there's company for tea
Ma spends hours instructing me
How to eat an' what to say.
An' I can't go out to play
When I've finished, but must stay
Till Ma whispers: " Now you may! "
Sittin' still is not much fun
When you've got your supper done.

When there's company for tea,
Then the servant waits on me
Last instead of first, an' I
Mustn't talk when she comes by;
If the boys outside should call,
I don't answer 'em at all;
You'd never know that it was me
When there's company for tea.

When I Get Home

When I get home at night they run
    To meet me down the street;
The duties of the day are done
    And joy is mine to meet.
Here is a welcome warm and true,
Worth every task a man can do.

I stoop to catch them in my arms
    And nestle face to face;
The finest of this old world's charms
    Is naught to this embrace;
Thus to be greeted, I declare,
Is worth a thousand years of care.

The toiling of the day is o'er,
    No more I need to roam,

They shout this through the open door:
  " Oh, Mother! Daddy's home! "
Who would not toil where engines hiss
To earn so glad an hour as this?

When I get home at night and see
  The little place aglow
With love and laughter all for me,
  The table set just so,
I tell myself, just one glad smile
Makes all the care of day worth while.

Oh, we have grieved and we have wept
  And bitter were our tears,
Yet when the long faith we have kept
  Through all the lonely years,
There will be glad souls in the gloam
To welcome us when we get home.

Living with the People

Living with the people, the good, the brave, the
    strong,
Glad to pass the time of day with all who come
    along.
Lord, it's good to meet Your children as they
    trudge life's thoroughfare,
And learn the hopes they cherish and the dreams
    they see out there.

Living with the people here upon the kindly
    earth,
And finding in the strangest garb the messengers
    of mirth,
For many a stirring tale of life the passer-by
    can tell,
And every man is worth your while if but you
    know him well.

Living with the people, the rich, the poor, the
    wise,
The same breeze blowing over them, the same
    sun in their eyes;
And this you learn from high and low, through-
    out life's stretch of years,
We're brothers in the joys we take and brothers
    in our tears.

I'm sorry for the haughty man who holds his
      head in air,
And passes by in cold disdain the garbs of toil
      and care,
For though he may be rich and great, 'tis lonely
      he must live,
He misses all the glorious joys his fellows have
      to give.

Oh, walk with them and talk with them and hear
      the tales they tell,
The passers-by would be your friends if but you
      knew them well.
The children of the Lord are they, and as they
      come and go,
There is not one among them all that is not good
      to know.

The Carving Knife

When I was but a little lad, my father carved
    what meat we had;
  With grace and skill he'd cut and slice the
    roast of beef or veal,
With dexterous hand he'd wield the blade, no
    false or awkward move he made,
  And deftly he could whet the knife upon his
    shining steel.
But now and then I'd hear him say: "Who's
    used my carving knife today?
  What woman's used this blade of mine for
    cutting wire or tin?"
And on this special point he'd harp: "a carv-
    ing weapon must be sharp,
  Or one can never cut a roast and have the
    slices thin."

"That knife must not be used on string, or
    bread or boards or anything —
  Hands off my carving blade," he'd cry, and
    yet I grieve to say,
In spite of all his warnings grim, the women paid
    no heed to him,
  They used his sacred carving knife a dozen
    times a day.
They'd use that knife for cutting soap, old car-
    pets, leather belts and rope,

They'd use it too, for pulling tacks and leave
  it dulled and nicked,
And every time a meal began, my father was
  an angry man,
  But vain was every oath he swore and every
  kick he kicked.

Now like my good old dad I stand, and take the
  carving knife in hand
  And run my thumb along its edge and find it
  dulled and nicked,
And like my good old dad I vow some day
  there'll be a healthy row,
  But I'm as unsuccessful as my father when
  he kicked.
The maid, the youngsters and the wife still take
  that sacred carving knife
  And use it as a handy tool on wood or lead or
  stone;
In spite of all I do or say, the blade is dulled
  from day to day,
  I cannot get the women folks to leave that
  knife alone!

Take a Boy Along With You

Take a boy along with you
And you'll learn before you're through
That this world is full of wonders
   You'd forgotten all about;
Song birds nesting in a tree
That you pass and never see,
Strange and curious mysteries
   The lad keeps pointing out.

He will question how and why,
With his bright and eager eye
He'll discover curious sights
   All along the way;
He'll show novelties to you
Which were hidden from your view,
And will fill with ecstasy
   Just a common day.

What to you is dull and old,
He will wonderingly behold,
Marvelous your dreary world
   Will appear to him;
And at every bend and turn
From that youngster you will learn
Just how much a man may miss
   When his eyes grow dim.

Who should say the world is bare,
Commonplace and filled with care?
Tired age may utter this,
    Blinded to its joy;
Sage and cynic, grown severe,
May have lost the magic here,
But the world is glorious
    To a little boy.

If you fancy life is just
Bearing burdens, as you must,
City streets and buildings tall
    And the moving throng,
If you've lost the power to see
Splendors as they used to be,
Some day when you're starting out
    Take a boy along.

When the Soap Gets in Your Eye

My father says that I ought to be
A man when anything happens to me.
An' he says that a man will take a blow
An' never let on it hurts him so;
He'll grit his teeth an' he'll set his chin
An' bear his pain with a manly grin.
But I'll bet that the bravest man would cry
If ever the soap gets into his eye.

I'm brave enough when I'm playin' ball,
An' I can laugh when I've had a fall.
With the girls around I'd never show
That I was scared if the blood should flow
From my banged up nose or a battered knee.
As brave as the bravest I can be,
But it's different pain, an' I don't know why,
Whenever the soap gets into your eye.

I can set my teeth an' I can grin
When I scrape my cheek or I bark my shin,
An' once I fell from our apple tree
An' the wind was knocked right out of me,
But I never cried an' the gang all said
That they thought for sure I was really dead.
But it's worse than thinking you're going to die
Whenever the soap gets into your eye.

When your mother's holding your neck, and you
Couldn't get away if you wanted to,
An' she's latherin' hard with her good right hand,
It's more than the bravest man could stand.
If you open your mouth to howl, you get
A taste of the wash rag, cold and wet,
But you got to yell till your face gets dry
Whenever the soap gets into your eye.

"Our Little House"

I'd like to have them think of me
As one with whom they liked to be;
I'd like to make my home so fair
That they would all be happy there;
To have them think, when life is done,
That here they had their finest fun.

Within these walls with love aglow,
They live to-morrow's "Long Ago."
Nor is the time so far away
When now shall be their yesterday,
And they shall turn once more to see
The little home which used to be

When comes that time I want them then
To wish they could be here again;
I want their memories to be
A picture of a kindly me,
To have them say how very glad
Their youthful lives were made by dad.

I want them to recall this place
As one of charm and tender grace,
To love these walls of calm content
Wherein their youthful years were spent,
And feel through each succeeding year,
They lived their happiest moments here.

I feel I shall have failed unless
This house shall shelter happiness.
Save they shall find their truest mirth
Around their father's humble hearth,
And here life's finest joys attain,
I shall have lived my life in vain.

Spring Fever

When the blue gets back in the skies once more
And the vines grow green 'round the kitchen
      door,
When the roses bud and the robins come,
I stretch myself and I say: "Ho-hum!
I ought to work but I guess I won't;
Though some want riches to-day, I don't;
This looks to me like the sort of day
That was made to idle and dream away."

When the sun is high and the air just right,
With the trees all blossomy, pink and white,
And the grass, as soft as a feather bed
With the white clouds drifting just overhead,
I stretch and yawn like a school boy then,
And turn away from the walks of men
And tell myself in a shamefaced way:
" I'm going to play hookey from work to-day!"

" Here is a morning too rare to miss,
And what is gold to a day like this,
And what is fame to the things I'll see
Through the lattice-work of a fine old tree?

There is work to do, but the work can wait;
There are goals to reach, there are foes to hate,
There are hurtful things which the smart might
    say,
But nothing like that shall spoil to-day."

" To-day I'll turn from the noisy town
And just put all of my burdens down;
I'll quit the world and its common sense,
And the things men think are of consequence,
To chum with birds and the friendly trees
And try to fathom their mysteries,
For here is a day which looks to be
The kind I can fritter away on me."

Father Song

It's oh, my little laddie, as you're romping at
    your play
There's an old heart running with you every
    minute of the day;
And though you cannot see me when you're
    wrapped up in a game,
But it's I that am beside you in your striving just
    the same.

It is oh, my little laddie, there is much you can-
    not know,

But it's I that follow proudly everywhere you
chance to go;
There's a hand upon your shoulder, wheresoever
you may be,
That would help you out of danger, and that
hand belongs to me.

It is oh, my little laddie, though you cannot hear
me call,
I am always there to help you every time you
chance to fall;
I am with you in the school room and I'm with
you on the street,
And though you may not know it, I am dogging
at your feet.

It's oh, my little laddie, all my life belongs to
you,
All the dreams that I have cherished through
the years depend on you;
And though now you cannot know it, you shall
some day come to see
How this old heart loved to hover 'round a boy
that used to be.

The Boy

A possible man of affairs,
  A possible leader of men,
Back of the grin that he wears
  There may be the courage of ten;
Lawyer or merchant or priest,
  Artist or singer of joy,
This, when his strength is increased,
  Is what may become of the boy.

Heedless and mischievous now,
  Spending his boyhood in play,
Yet glory may rest on his brow
  And fame may exalt him some day;
A skill that the world shall admire,
  Strength that the world shall employ
And faith that shall burn as a fire,
  Are what may be found in the boy.

He with the freckles and tan,
  He with that fun-loving grin,
May rise to great heights as a man
  And many a battle may win;
Back of the slang of the streets
  And back of the love of a toy,
It may be a Great Spirit beats —
  Lincoln once played as a boy.

Trace them all back to their youth,
　　All the great heroes we sing,
Seeking and serving the Truth,
　　President, poet and king,
Washington, Caesar and Paul,
　　Homer who sang about Troy,
Jesus, the Greatest of all,
　　Each in his time was a boy.

I Don't Want to Go to Bed

World wide over this is said:
"I don't want to go to bed."
Dads and mothers, far and near,
Every night this chorus hear;
Makes no difference where they are,
Here or off in Zanzibar,
In the igloos made of snow
Of the fur-clad Eskimo,
In this blistering torrid zone,
This one touch of nature's known;
In life's various tongues it's said:
"I don't want to go to bed!"

This has ever been the way
Of the youngsters at their play.
Laughter quickly dries their tears,
Trouble swiftly disappears,

Joy is everywhere about,
Here and there and in and out;
Yet when night comes on they cry
That so glad a day should die,
And they think that they will miss
Something more of precious bliss,
So shouts every curly-head:
" I don't want to go to bed! "

Age is glad to put away
All the burdens of the day,
Glad to lay the worries down,
Quit the noises of the town,
And in slumber end the care
That has met them here and there.
But the children do not know
Life is freighted down with woe;
They would run until they drop,
Hoping day would never stop,
Calling back when it has fled:
" I don't want to go to bed."

Morning Brigands

There may be happier times than this,
  But if there are I've never known them,
When youngsters jump in bed to kiss
  And wake the pa's and ma's who own them.
What if the sun be up or not,
  Another perfect day is dawning,
And is it not a happy lot
  With such delight to greet the morning?

Sometimes I hear them quit their bed
  And catch their bare-foot pitter-patter,
And other times they're at my head
  Before I know what is the matter.
Brigands to rob us of our sleep
  They come—their weapons love and laughter,
And though we're locked in slumber deep,
  They always get the joy they're after.

Some days there are when we would lie
  And dream our dreams a little longer,
Then "back to bed awhile," we cry —
  But oh, our love for them is stronger,
Yes, stronger than our wish to sleep
  And so we countermand the order
And let that pair of brigands leap
  With wild delight across love's border.

There may be happier times than this,
 But if there are I've never known them,
When youngsters jump in bed to kiss
 And wake the pa's and ma's who own them.
They miss a lot, the man and wife
 Who never feel those glad hands shake them,
Who rise by day to toil and strife,
 But have no little tots to wake them.

Grief's Only Master

Into the lives of all
The tears of sorrow fall.
Into the happiest hearts
Grief drives her darts;
No door however stout
Can shut Death's angel out.

Vain are the things we prize,
Treasure and pomp's disguise;
They cannot stay the tear
When the true griefs appear.
Where Death will strike to-day
Gold cannot bar the way.

There is no joy secure,
No peace that shall endure,
No smile that man shall keep.

God wills that he must weep,
And in his darkest hour
Vain is all earthly power.

What, then, should guard the gate?
How shall a man be great?
Through the dark days and long,
What power shall make him strong?
Wherein does courage lie,
Since all he loves must die?

When sorrow binds his hands,
Helpless the strong man stands.
One master only grief
Bows to, and that's belief —
Faith that he'll some day know
Why God hath willed it so!

INDEX OF FIRST LINES